Red Green's

[Duct Tape Is Not Enough]

A Humorous Guide to Midlife

Red Green's

[Duct Tape Is Not Enough]

A Humorous Guide to Midlife

Steve Smith

Illustrated by Bryce Hallett

Hatherleigh Press
New York

Red Green's Duct Tape Is Not Enough
A Hatherleigh Press Book

Published by Hatherleigh Press
An Affiliate of W.W. Norton and Company, Inc.
5-22 46th Avenue, Suite 200
Long Island City, NY 11101
Toll Free 1-800-528-2550
Visit our website, hatherleighpress.com

Hatherleigh Press books are available for bulk purchase, special promotions and premiums. For more information on reselling and special purchase opportunities, please call us at 1-800-528-2550 and ask for the Special Sales Manager.

Library of Congress Cataloging-in-Publication Data

Smith, Steve, 1945-
    Red Green's duct tape is not enough : a humorous guide to midlife / Steve Smith;
illustrated by Bryce Hallett.
        p. cm.
    Companion book to the television show, the Red Green Show.
    ISBN 1-57826-109-0 (pbk.)
    1. Canadian wit and humor. 2. Middle age—Humor. 3. Aging—Humor. I. Title: Duct tape is not enough. II. Hallet, Bryce. III. Red Green Show. IV. Title.

PN6178.C3 S655 2002
814'.54—dc21   2002019104

Cover Design by Mick Andreano Designs
Interior Design and Layout by Fatema Tarzi

10 9 8 7 6 5 4 3 2 1
Printed on acid-free paper.
Printed in Canada

THANKS...

to all of the readers of my column, *North of Forty*,
and all of the viewers of *The Red Green Show*,
and especially to all of the members of Possum Lodge.

—*Red Green*

FOREWORD

Thank you for buying this book. (Even if you stole it, there's promotional value for me, assuming your inmates will eventually be paroled.) The only downside here is that this book represents a monumental conflict of interest for me. My television show relies heavily on duct tape. My first feature film is called *Duct Tape Forever* (see color section.) I even have my own brand of duct tape—The Handyman's Secret Weapon★. The concept of my suggesting that duct tape has a shortcoming is difficult for me personally and professionally. On the other hand, I've been writing a syndicated newspaper column about the middle-aged experience for the last few years, and since you write about what you know, I have to confess that I have much more in common with a middle-aged married guy than I do with a roll of duct tape. And although duct tape is capable of doing more jobs than any other creation in the history of human endeavor, for anyone in the throes of that period of enlightenment known as midlife, sadly, duct tape is NOT enough.

—*Red Green*

★A Scotch 3M Product

CARPE DUCTUM
(SEIZE THE TAPE)

—RED GREEN

The Younger Woman Thing

I bumped into an old buddy I hadn't seen since high school. He's just remarried, and his new wife is 27 years younger than he is. Naturally, when you see something like that, it's only human nature to ask yourself, "Why him?" Or even more courageously, "Why not me?" And how does a guy in his 50s meet a 25-year-old woman in the first place? Maybe when she picked up her parents from bridge club.

I try to picture it: a wispy young thing is having a latte at the Second Cup when a middle-aged balding fat guy comes over and says, "Maybe we should go out sometime."

And then she says, "Sounds like fun."

Hunh?? It's all too surreal for me.

So, you guys out there with wives your own age, you're the real men. Anybody can impress a naïve young thing. It's a lot harder to tough it out with a woman who's been around the block a few times. A woman who's gone to bed with you for the last 30 years. And is planning to be there again tonight. Unless she meets some 90-year-old smooth talker at the Second Cup.

Confidence Can Kill

Sometimes, when a man reaches middle age, he gets a little full of himself. Maybe he's been reasonably successful at work, has a nice home and family, and hasn't raised any convicted felons, and he starts thinking that he knows it all. This ticks off everyone around him and ironically, he's the last one to notice. So watch for these signs that indicate you're getting obnoxious:

- People at work volunteer you for a climb of Mt. Everest.

- When you talk to neighbors they run away, pretending to hear their phones ring.

- On Valentine's Day, you're given a box of prunes.

- Your wife insists that when the two of you travel, you go on separate planes.

- The other guys in your car pool kick the muffler off your car so they can't hear what you're saying.

- Your best friend works for Amway but has never tried to sell you anything.

- When the firemen arrive the first thing they do is hose you down, even though the burning building is across the street.

- Whenever you talk at a party, your wife sits behind you shaking her head.

How Connected Are You?

Like most people my age, I've been dragged kicking and screaming into the age of technology. Including the world of Internet and e-mail and the reclassification of the disadvantaged to include people with only one phone line. I don't know what software you're using, but the stuff I'm on gives my connection rate whenever I go online. It says, "You're connected at 44,000 BPS," or 37,000 BPS or whatever. This affects the speed at which I can download information. So I'm thinking this would be a handy thing to flash on an unseen screen in the back of my mind when I meet a new person at a party. If it says, "You are connected at 3 BPS," I would know to speak slowly to this person, keep it simple and move on as quickly as possible. If on the other hand it says, "You are connected at 3,000,000 BPS," I better pay attention and keep it interesting and move the conversation on as quickly as possible. I would also consider this person as a potential life partner. Except for the fact that I'm already married—and when it comes to the connection speed with my wife, we're on cable.

Will As Payback Time

As the bunch of us gets older, we're seeing more commercials for wills. How to prepare them. Why to have them. What to put in them. I don't think wills are used to their full potential. First of all, don't try to say how much you care about people in your will. It just makes them feel bad. They don't need to read it from you after you're gone—they need to hear it from you while you're still around. To me the true fun is to use your will to make people improve themselves. For example, you can leave your riding mower to your neighbor provided he returns the hedge clippers he borrowed from you in 1973—and it has to be the exact pair—you kept a picture. You can leave your barbecue to the people up the street provided they camp in your backyard listening to their dog bark all night as you did for so many years. You can leave five thousand dollars to the city provided they repave the street like they promised to in the last municipal election. You get the idea. Have some fun with it. A will is your last chance to make a point—and nobody can talk back.

The Art of Avoiding Conversation

Here are 5 Survival Tips on how to keep a marriage smoking long after the fire has gone out.

- **Be very quiet when she's talking.** If she stops talking, always wait a full minute before speaking: she may not be finished.

- **Do not change the subject.** Even if you have to speak first, you can usually figure out what she wants to talk about. For example, if she's trying to clean an oil stain on the kitchen floor, she probably wants to talk about you trying to fix the lawnmower in the sink.

- **Watch her body language.** Alter what you're saying in response to what she does. If she stops doing her nails and starts sharpening a knife, it's time for you to do a 180.

- **Maintain eye contact.** If you can't see her eyes, you have no idea how things are going. If you're working on the car and she asks you about plans for the weekend, take the time to roll out on the creeper so you can see her response rather than just yelling, "I'm going fishing with Bob. I told you that last week" from under the car. Remember: she has access to heavy tools and the lower half of your body is exposed. Always maintain eye contact. Don't have conversations in the dark and don't talk to your wife on the telephone unless you're a professional.

- **Keep your sentences short.** Five words maximum. That allows you to change direction quickly if it's not going well. You can say "Unless" or "But" or "Whatever." Short sentences give her a chance to talk. Which is what you want. You want the conversation to go her way. It's not about success. It's about survival.

Quote of the Day

"If you find that time goes by too fast, spend an hour with a boring relative."

—*Red Green*

Dances with Disaster

There are a lot of things a man can do to fool everybody as to his true age. There are a number of products out there to help. Hair dyes and wrinkle cream, cosmetic surgery and toupees, contact lenses, laxatives and Viagra. You can talk about things that younger people talk about. You can wear young clothes and drive a young person's car. You can even pretend to like young people's music. But it's all over when you hit the dance floor. Once you start flailing away doing the Frug or the Monkey or the Locomotion, you've blown your cover. When people see you dance they know you grew up with Chubby Checker. Even slow dances give you away. With your arm stuck straight out like a railway crossing gate. The horrible truth is that you have to make a choice. You must either be honest about your age or never ever ever dance. It's a tough one. My advice is to do both.

Quote of the Day

"Monster Trucks are for people who don't understand wrestling."

—*Red Green*

The Whole World in Your Hands

I find that, generally, women like to keep souvenirs and pictures and mementos a lot more than men do. We probably have half a dozen photo albums and boxes of kids' paintings in our house. Most men don't need that stuff. They can take a trip down memory lane just by looking at their own hands. Take a few minutes on a Saturday morning and look at your hands. Turn them over slowly so you can see all the scars and nicks, and it's amazing how the memories will come flooding back. How can you look at that thumbnail without remembering the dock you built and then rebuilt and then hired a guy to rebuild who charged too much because he'd seen your work? When you notice the one with the missing hair, it reminds you which hand you use to light the barbecue. Some of the marks bring back simple images—a chainsaw, a Cuisinart, a nail gun. Some of them remind you of locations—up on the roof looking down, followed immediately by down on the ground looking up—under the car—inside the furnace—over the steam valve—inside the ambulance. But you don't want to look back too much. So drop your hands, pick up your toolbox, have a couple of aspirins, and go make some memories.

Psychologist, Heal Thyself

I have a couple of concerns about the whole self-help movement thing. The idea is that each of us is great and fantastic and there's nothing we can't do if we just liberate ourselves from negative thoughts. I'm 53 years old, twenty pounds overweight, and barely average height, with poor eye-hand coordination and a history of avoiding physical exertion. No amount of self-help will allow me to be the starting center for the Chicago Bulls. And that's not just a negative thought, it's also a positive reality. The point is, we need to have negative thoughts about ourselves. Negative thoughts keep us employed and married and allow us to get along with our friends and neighbors. Nothing kills a relationship faster than saying to yourself, "I could do better." Especially when the truth is, "They could do better." Try to think of your ego as a hot air balloon. The positive thoughts keep it up, the negative thoughts keep it down. The perfect altitude for you is just above the high-tension wires and just below the radar. Too many positive thoughts and you have too far to fall. Too many negative thoughts and you're dragging your basket.

Grey Horsepower

I was driving into the city yesterday and I was speeding. I was at least twenty percent over the speed limit and I went right by a parked police car, but he didn't chase me or signal me or pull me over. That's because I was pretty much the slowest car on the road. Everybody speeds now. The average car today goes much faster than the average car of thirty years ago. Yet the average driver today is much older than the average driver of thirty years ago. Does that make sense to you? That as our population ages, we think it's a good idea to give them more horsepower? Think about your own grandfather—his eyesight, his hearing, his reaction time, his alertness, his sleepy leg. Please don't allow him to be at the wheel of a speeding car. You must put the safety of others ahead of your impatience for the inheritance.

Quote of the Day

"Let sleeping dogs lie. Let waking men exaggerate."

—*Red Green*

No Peaking

A lot of guys I know have a photograph of themselves in great physical shape. Maybe they were on the rowing team or maybe they were running every day or maybe they just had the time and motivation to work out on a regular basis. So they have this picture of themselves with small waists and rippling muscles. It might be on their desks or somewhere in their homes or, even worse, buried deep in their minds. Every time they see or even think about that picture, they are reminded of how the aging process has destroyed them. It's been a constant deterioration from that earlier peak of physical prowess to the pitiful flabby lethargic bald specimen they have now become.

I, on the other hand, have a picture of myself on the beach at the age of 13. My weight was within ten pounds of what it is now and there is no physical evidence of any type of muscle. I can stand beside that picture at any time and comfort myself that I have not "started to sag" or "let myself go" or "lost a step." I was out of shape at 13 and I've maintained it all these years. Nobody looks at my picture and says, "Wow, is that you?" Instead of looking good for a year or two and then feeling bad my whole life, I opted for looking bad all the time and feeling good my whole life.

Get It in Writing

The engineers keep coming up with new gadgets, and then the salesmen have to figure out why we have to have them. It's called technology in search of a market. Well, I think I can help. I saw this gadget recently. It's like a little computerized Dictaphone that you talk into, and it converts what you say into text that you can read. The words come up on a little screen and you can print them off or save them on your computer or just look at them and marvel at your own genius. I have a great application for this product. Instead of using it on yourself, use it to record what other people say. Everybody's pretty fast and loose with oral communication, but there's a healthy respect for the written word. Just think if you could have recorded your wife's voice that one time in your twenty-year marriage when you both knew you were right. Or that time your boss got into the eggnog and promised you a job for life. Wouldn't it be a great way to immortalize what you've been told? Expressions like "Your car will be ready by three o'clock" or "Your home will never go down in value" or "Don't worry, I'm sure it's just a mole."

Birds Have Wings for a Reason

Able-bodied children who stay at home past the age of adulthood are going against the fundamental Laws of Nature. In the world of animals, the kids get a year, two years tops, and then they are outta there. If I had adult kids, I would compare our family to a family of birds. Your mother and I had you in the nest where we hatched you and fed you. If you want to stay out there on your own, fine, but if you want to come back to the nest, your mother and I will be sitting on you.

You're Not Getting Older, You're Getting More Focused

Some people see the aging process as the law of diminishing returns. I prefer to look at it as Nature's way of coordinating knowledge, experience and focus. As you lose your hair and vision and hearing and libido and general degree of attractiveness to members of the opposite sex, or any sex, of any species, you're left to concentrate on your true purpose in life. I'm still not completely sure what that is, but for me it's trending toward some combination of eating junk food, watching television and complaining. I'm sure I'll have a clearer picture any day now. I'll keep you posted.

Quote of the Day

"Water seeks its own level. Booze goes straight to the head."

—Red Green

Ten Signs That You Are Non-Communicative

- When you phone somebody, you're hoping to get their voice-mail.

- You never ask anyone a question because you have no interest in their answer.

- When you have a passenger in your car, you turn the radio up as loud as it will go.

- You spend a lot of time alone in the garage.

- When you have something to say, you speak loudly without taking a pause and then quickly exit the room.

- E-mail is your favorite method of communicating because you can say whatever you want without interruption and then delete the reply without reading it.

- When you come upon someone walking in the street, instead of saying "Good morning" you pretend to see something important in the distance and start running towards it.

- Your office phone has been set on Voice Message since 1991.

- On the rare occasion when you send greeting cards, you don't sign them.

- You wear headphones that aren't plugged into anything.

The Shrinking Attention Span

click
click
click

I'll try to keep this short. I find that guys my age have a short attention span. I'm not saying that's bad. In fact, most of the time, it's a good thing. We're starting to sense that time is running out and we don't want to waste it reading thick books or watching mini-series or listening to the neighbor talk about her cats.

We like short, pithy, meaningful sound bites. People that attempt to communicate with us need to accept that and to alter their style of communication to fit those parameters. Here's a short checklist I make people ask themselves before they waste my precious time:

- Do I know you?

- Does this information affect me personally and will not having it cause me bodily harm or, worse still, cost me money?

- Can you express your thought in less than ten seconds?

- Are you planning to use words that I don't know?

- Will you be blocking the exit?

The Young and the Useless

Our local television station was doing one of those success profiles of a guy in town who had made a gazillion dollars and had women sending in resumes in hopes of having his children. I found the whole thing mildly irritating, but I really lost it when they announced that this guy was 27 years old. No average man over the age of forty needs to hear that. If they can make a v-chip that filters out sex and violence, they should be able to invent a gizmo that prevents the viewer from learning that not only is most of the world doing better than him, they're also doing it at half his age. Maybe they could even make a thingee that substitutes a higher, more palatable number whenever age is mentioned. Wouldn't it be great to hear that Bill Gates was 87 or Ricky Martin was 63 or Mark McGwire was 74? It would give us all hope for the future.

Quote of the Day

"I move slowly because I'm not sure where I'm going."

—*Red Green*

Taking a Flyer

I was on a flight last week and I was watching the stewardess do her seatbelt–emergency exit–oxygen mask routine… Can I still say "stewardess"? Or is it "flight attendant" or "high hostess" or "pretzel person" now? Whatever she was, she wasn't a very young version of it. She was about my age. My mind went back about thirty years to when stewardesses had to be young and good-looking and single. I think it was because there was no movie. The stewardess was the entertainment. She was also the liaison between the airline and the customer. She was sweet and accommodating and had that air of availability that kept the businessmen on the edges of their seats with their tray tables in the full upright position. How times have changed. Now we've got a matronly sergeant major with a smoker's cough and a big attitude. I used to watch the seatbelt demonstration because I wanted to. Now I'm afraid she'll cuff me one if I look away. And she's probably married to someone like me, so I can't fool her. Equal opportunity has taken all the fun out of flying.

Guilty by Association

I know movie stars and athletes make a lot of money doing endorsements for running shoes or phone companies, but what we're seeing now is getting out of hand. Bob Dole pitching for Viagra. Karl Malone of the Utah Jazz selling Rogaine. Come on, guys, where's your pride? I would never do either of those. It's an insult even to be asked. Can you imagine being approached by a laxative company because they think you truly represent what their product is all about? Television ads and billboards all over the country with your face right next to the word "bowel." Is that the kind of fame you want? People recognizing you and then crossing to the other side of the street? Going to a restaurant and being seated near the restroom? It can't be worth it.

How Men and Women Work

It's always helpful to identify the difference between men and women in the interest of universal peace and global warming. To that end, I've noticed that men and women generally have a different approach to work. Women are doers. Men are delegators. Women pride themselves on maximizing their own personal productivity. Men pride themselves on getting someone else to do the job. That's why women are hands-on while men prefer power tools. We're programmed for work avoidance. It's not our fault.

The human reproductive process is the model for all other forms of man-woman interaction. The man is there for the first five minutes for all the fun and excitement, and at the end of the meeting, the woman takes sole responsibility for the project for the next nine months.

Quote of the Day

"Never carry gasoline in your car trunk unless it's in a container of some kind."

—*Red Green*

The Specialization Age

Many experts advise us to fight the aging process. They tell us that we need a disciplined diet and a rigorous exercise regimen, and that this will somehow keep us young. This to me is fighting the fundamental rules of Nature. The world does not need you to stay young. We have young people who are much more willing and able to do that job. So instead of trying to take the place of a younger, healthier person, why don't you try to find the place that has been reserved for you? You can find that place by looking at yourself and focusing on your strengths. You may not hear very well, which is Nature's way of telling you to listen more. You may not see very well, which is Nature's way of telling you not to look. You may have lost a lot of strength and speed, which is Nature's way of telling you to sit down before you kill yourself. Maybe you could even cheer somebody else on. Your memory is fading, which is Nature's way of preventing you from holding a grudge. You've spent a lot of years taking in information, which means you're in a great position to draw some conclusions on life, before life draws a conclusion on you. Sure you're getting older, but you can also get better. You just can't get younger. Step away from those roller blades. Now.

Nine Signs You're Taking Each Other for Granted

- In a group photo taken recently, you have trouble picking out your wife.

- You drive in the car for three hours without speaking and that's fine with her.

- The cancellation of Wheel of Fortune would create a depressing void in both of your lives.

- For your anniversary, you bought her the exact same ball cap you bought her last year. And she didn't notice.

- Your wife discusses your medical condition with her friends while you're present and then wants you to show them the scar.

- You can use your meals as a calendar. Meat Loaf is Monday; Chicken is Tuesday; McDonald's is Payday…

- A sit-down dinner at your house involves TV trays.

- On a night when you're working late, you call home to tell her and that makes her suspicious.

- Neither of you goes to bed until you're really really tired.

Kissing Butt Meets a Tragic End

The new corporate operating policies are really messing with the "suck up" system that was firmly established during the development of the industrialized world. It used to be that you would come in at an entry level position in someone's department, like say Howard's department, and then you would curry favor with Howard over the next ten years, following him up the corporate ladder until he eventually retired and you replaced him. You weren't an independent isolated employee. You were "Howard's man." You were protected. These days it's just the opposite. They gave Howard the golden handshake to replace him with a 23-year-old whiz-bang who's going to turn the whole department on its ear and you're a problem. You're "Howard's man." You have knowledge and experience which makes you "out of it." So you're gone too. Corporations today are much more comfortable with a guy who doesn't know anything than with a guy who knows too much.

A Middle-Aged Man's Wallet

Many of us have several ad hoc living time capsules that show the chronology of our lives. One of them is our wallets. If you found a wallet and it had these things in it, you'd know it belonged to a middle-aged guy:

- A picture of Charo.

- Ticket stubs from a Herman's Hermits concert.

- An unused condom marked "Best Before April 12, 1965."

- The condom is wrapped around a Viagra pill.

- A picture of a man in his early twenties wearing the exact same leisure suit that the wallet owner is currently wearing.

- A large collection of business cards of varying age. They are all from radically different businesses, although they all have the wallet owner's name on them.

- A small calendar identifying the owner's time-share week in Greenland.

- The singed remains of his Ford Pinto Proof of Ownership.

- A coupon to have his colors done.

- No money.

Less Really Is More

I went shopping for some new pants last week. I haven't measured my waist in a while but I know there's been growth in that area because I can feel more parts of the chair rubbing against my sides and back. So I grabbed a few pairs to try on ranging in size between 40 and 44. Well holy cow, they were all too big. And I mean way too big. I ended up with a size 34. Size 34. I wore a size 34 when I was in high school. I'm doing fine. I'm in shape.

Well it just so happens I still have a pair of pants from high school up in the attic so I went up to try them on. It didn't go well. I'm not sure if I could have done up the waist or not since I couldn't get the pants past the mid-thigh region. Could these pants—these tuxedo pants that haven't been washed, ever, and haven't been to the cleaners since I spilled that Baby Duck at the prom—could these pants have shrunk in the attic? No. I think we all know the horrible truth. They've changed the sizes. The reason I don't have to take a Size 42 is because a Size 34 *is* a Size 42. And not for all pants. Not for young pants like the ones your kids wear. No, these pants I just bought are targeted as old-guy-big-butt pants. They size them liberally because guys don't need another reason not to buy clothes. Especially old guys. With big butts.

Driving Mrs. Daisy

You can tell how long a couple has been married just by watching them drive their car:

- If he's driving and she's cuddled up close, they are newlyweds. They also have to have an old car to be able to sit that close. That also proves they're newlyweds.

- If she's driving and he's cuddled up close, they've been married for a few years and he's in a little trouble. Alcohol may be involved. Especially if they have bucket seats.

- If he's driving and she's sitting way over on the other side, as far away as she can get, they've been married at least five years and he has forced her to leave the mall before she was ready.

- If he's driving and she's speaking heatedly to him and pointing out directions with her hands, they've been married ten years.

- If he's driving and she's not speaking to him at all, they've been married eleven years.

- If he's driving and she's sitting in the back seat, they've been married fifteen years. If he's wearing a cap, he's also had a serious demotion.

- If they're driving separate cars, they've been married twenty years.

- If she's driving and he's walking, they're divorced.

My Second Cup Runneth Over

One of the signs that our society is changing is the decline in the number of taverns in the community and the proliferation of coffee bars. They have them in malls, at airports, even in bookstores. Is this really a good idea? We have a population that's over-worked and over-stressed. Is more caffeine a good thing? I wonder how much of the end of civility in our society is directly attributable to that fourth cup of java. Road rage, arguments over a parking spot, jockeying for position when lining up—none of these situations is improved by the presence of Juan Valdez. When I see a guy on the news climbing the bell tower with an assault rifle, I wonder if things might have been different if he'd switched to decaf.

Before Best Before

When I was growing up we didn't have "Best Before" stickers on anything. If the milk smelled okay, you drank it. If the meat was somewhere in the vicinity of its original color, you ate it. If the can only had rust on the outside, you ate the contents. That doesn't happen anymore. And we didn't have big egos back then, so even if that tub of ice cream was "Best Before January 12th", that implied that it was still good on January 13th, and good was good enough for us. Those days are gone. Now everyone demands the best. That's why people will sit up all night finishing off the ice cream before it goes bad the next day. And they wonder why we're all overweight. I was wondering if this "Best Before" concept will expand to include friends and family. Can you picture Uncle Ernie with a sticker saying "Best Before Second Martini" or Grandpa's saying "Best Before 7 p.m." or your own saying "Best Before 1971"?

Quote of the Day

"He who laughs last had to wait for the stitches to come out."

—*Red Green*

The Truth As We Know It

Has this ever happened to you? You're out with your spouse at a social function and they start pontificating on a topic about which they know nothing. Coincidentally it's often a topic about which you know a great deal—your business or your investment or you personally. And what's worse, they're making all kinds of false statements and exaggerations. If you've only been married a short time, there's a temptation to correct your spouse in front of others. You will soon learn that not only does the truth hurt, but also that it's usually a self-inflicted wound. So don't ever correct your partner in a group. Neither should you stand behind him or her and make hand gestures that indicate to the others that you think your spouse is a little bit wacko. No, your job is to move away slowly or pretend you're not listening or act drunk. The truth is for church or the courts. When the truth comes out at parties, it's only going to make trouble.

Too Old to Be Loose

I was sitting in an airport last week and over on the corner of the waiting area was a couple of teenagers lying on the floor sleeping. They were using coats as blankets and backpacks as pillows. And nobody was bothering them or even making comments. It was just accepted that these were a couple of normal sleep-deprived kids off to see the world. And I couldn't help wondering what the response would have been if they were middle-aged men lying there, rather than teenagers. I'm guessing "not good." Society doesn't approve of men sleeping on the floor in a public place. Not even married men. It's a question of leeway. As we get older, our leeway shrinks. A teenager with the crotch of his pants down around his knees is a hip-hop happening. When a middle-aged man does it, it's a citizen's arrest. Try to imagine a middle-aged guy hitch-hiking. Or caddying. Or dating your daughter. There's no leeway.

Quote of the Day

"Is that all there is? I hope so."

—*Red Green*

Ten Signs of an Uneven Balance of Power

We all know that the best relationships are close to a fifty-fifty partnership. Here are the signs that perhaps one partner is dominating the other.

- There is an old rusty car abandoned in the front yard.

- The husband and wife wear matching shirts.

- The family dog is a cat.

- The family vehicle is a motorcycle with a sidecar.

- The beer fridge is the one in the kitchen.

- One of them wears an "I'm with Stupid" t-shirt.

- One of them keeps the TV remote on their person.

- The welcome mat says "Trespassers will be shot."

- The lawn is covered with cutouts of fat people bending over.

- There's a couch on the front porch. There's also a guy sleeping on it.

Keep Your Shirt On

I like to watch football on TV, but I find that lately it's getting violent and offensive and the camera coverage is far too graphic. Of course I'm talking about those shots of inebriated fans with their shirts off. There was a guy on last night's game sporting a bad green-and-gold paint job on a gut so massive he must have used a roller or he would have been late for the game. And it's not enough that he has this overwhelming mass of unsaturated fat to share with us, he also feels that he needs to wave his arms frantically and jump up and down, making his belly look like an aerial video of a 7.2 earthquake.

Now, I know I talk a lot about how difficult it is to be married and to have to make compromises, but I think this is a situation where being married can really help. I'm talking to all of you fat guys out there. Before you go to the game, get your stomach all painted up and show it to your wife and ask her if she thinks the world wants or needs to see this. And please, please, listen to her answer. Some of us are watching the game with our families, perhaps having dinner in front of the TV. You must stop the madness.

The End of the End

I have a theory about the size of a man's butt. (I'm happy to report that I haven't done any research on this.) My theory is that, throughout a man's life, the size of his butt pretty much follows the pattern of the Bell Curve, starting out quite small, increasing in mass in the early teens, expanding exponentially through the thirties and forties, reaching the zenith of its growth potential around the age of 53, and then diminishing in size exponentially until the age of 75, at which time it has returned to being quite small. I can understand why it enlarges through middle age because there's usually a fairly substantial gut out front, and if the butt was too small, a man would be unbalanced and unable to stand up. But I don't understand why it has to shrink with age. It seems cruel or at least ironic that when you finally get to the age where you can stop worrying, you've got nothing to fall back on.

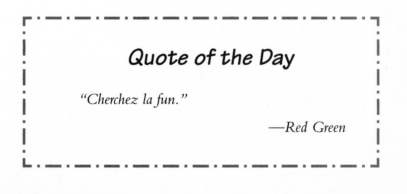

Quote of the Day

"Cherchez la fun."

—*Red Green*

My Stomach Is Killing Me (and vice versa)

I find that a lot of guys my age have trouble with their stomachs. What was once a low-priority and relatively maintenance-free part of their anatomy is now looming large, both physically and medically. I think the main problem is that most of us have no knowledge of, or respect for, how the stomach works. Here's my take on it. The stomach is where the food arrives and is mixed with chemicals that will break it down so that the body can burn it. In other words, the stomach is the carburetor of the body. Not the fuel injector. It can't handle high quantity intake no matter how big a supercharger your mouth is. And then there's the quality issue. You can't run a high performance engine, i.e. the human body, on chili dogs and draft beer. Once in a while, you need to fill up on high test (i.e. roughage). Something that will get you up and moving, at least during the halftime show. But the biggest problem with the stomach is that it's connected to the brain. If your mind is upset, your stomach will be too. The answer is to deal with whatever is troubling your mind and that will calm your stomach, rather than assaulting your stomach with deep-fried jalapenos hoping that will calm your mind.

Getting the Seniors' Discount

I was in a restaurant for lunch yesterday. One of those salad buffet places where you fill your plate with low calorie, no-fat lettuce and tomatoes and then smother it with mounds of creamy salad dressing and a couple of handfuls of bacon bits. So I'm standing there at the cash register in a "What a great day" kind of mood and the cashier says,

"Do you get the Seniors' Discount?"

"Say WHAT!?!"

"The Seniors' Discount?"

"Are you talking to me!?!"

I was so upset, I could barely go back for seconds. Okay, having a Seniors' Discount for people over 50 is a fine incentive for customers and all that—but they've got to handle it right. I'm 53 and, like most men my age, I think that I look about 37. I don't need some 19-year-old sweetie exploding that myth in front of total strangers. Not for a lousy 10 percent. My pride is worth at least 15.

Hitting Bottom in the Top Drawer

I had an unsettling revelation as I was getting dressed the other day. There was some new underwear in my drawer, still in the package. My wife had bought it for me. It's something she does once in a while. And I don't know why but I tried to think back to the last time I had bought my own underwear. I've been married 33 years so it was before that. And in the period between my wedding and high school, I just made do with what I had. I didn't buy any in high school either. Or in elementary school. And I didn't buy any before kindergarten. At that time, I was a rookie in the underwear department. And before that, I was in diapers. So the horrible truth hit me. I HAVE NEVER IN MY WHOLE LIFE BOUGHT MY OWN UNDERWEAR! I don't know what that means but I suspect it is somehow at the root of so many other problems in my life. If there is anybody out there in the same situation, perhaps we should get together and form a support group. Although if we could provide our own support, none of this would be necessary.

Life Is Sport

Now I know a lot of women like sports, but I think that, on a per capita basis, the vast majority of sports fans are men. And predominantly middle-aged men. We're the ones sprawled out on the family room couch with an ottoman handy to catch the overflow. We're the ones who will watch any sport, anytime, anywhere. And I think I know why. In sports you are always living "in the moment." While what happened in the past may have some relevance and what may happen in the future is tinged with hope, the main focus in sports is what is happening RIGHT NOW. Middle-aged men love that. That's where we want to be—living in the moment. Not living in the past when we had more of everything, from freedom to hairstyle choices, where we can be criticized for our uninspired career choices after graduation or our inappropriate behavior at last night's party. Not living in the future, where we will look back at our current physical deterioration as the good old days. No, we don't want to think about that. The truth is we don't want to think about anything. But hey, that's what sports on television is for.

He Who Dies with the Most Toys, Wins

I've spent most of my life first acknowledging, and then foolishly trying to identify, the differences between men and women. And I think a big one is their attitude towards toys. While both sexes may agree that toys are childish with no redeeming social value, women somehow see that as a bad thing. Or maybe it's the manufacturers' fault. They stop making toys for women once they hit puberty. With men, the process accelerates. It's just that the toys get bigger—speed boats, monster trucks, ATVs, radio controlled cars and planes, bulldozers, nuclear missiles, etc. Look around at the stores in your city. How many of them carry toys for women? I'm guessing there aren't any, except maybe Chippendale's. That's just not fair. In fact, it's sexism at its worst. I say the time has come to give women equal opportunity to be convinced of the value of toys. Then maybe my wife will let me buy that big screen.

Quote of the Day

"It's okay to be unreliable. Until you're alone... which you will be."

—Red Green

A Wise Bird Never Messes Its Own Nest

With the increasing amount of leisure time available to middle-aged couples over the last few years, we're all starting to expand our interests and hobbies and this is creating a real problem. Women are quilting and doing needlepoint and painting in acrylics and making dried floral arrangements. Men are doing woodwork and building model airplanes and renovating unused bedrooms and making lawn ornaments. Unfortunately very few of us are any good at this stuff. What we end up with is some butt-ugly thing that they make better with a machine in Taiwan and that costs about 99 cents and, more importantly, that you're allowed to throw in the garbage without starting World War III. Some people give their creations to their friends, but there's a risk of them returning the favor. So I say what we need are designated Hobby Centers set up by the government in abandoned schools or whatever. We would all go there on a Saturday morning and do our hobby thing—build or sew or paint, doesn't matter—and then when we're finished, and this is the important part, the thing that we made is NOT ALLOWED TO LEAVE THE BUILDING… EVER.

Signs That You're Ready to Retire

- You have toys in your desk.

- You carry your golf clubs in the back of your company vehicle. (Ambulance)

- You have lost your appetite for debt.

- Lately you've been buying a lot of slippers.

- You're dying your hair to make yourself look older.

- You leave work by 3:30 so you can take advantage of the early bird special.

- You comment to your boss on how much better the new guy is at doing your job.

- You're obsessed with your lawn.

- Your briefcase is full of brochures from Sarasota.

- You tried on a pair of pink pants with a white belt and you thought they looked sharp.

Being One with the Garage

A lot of guys my age have somewhere they can go where they can be alone and have peace and think or tinker around or whatever. Sometimes it's a club in town or a bowling alley or a bar. More often, it's a place in their own home. Sometimes a basement workshop or a garden shed but usually it's the garage. You'll see a guy's garage and he'll have an old couch and a TV and a beer fridge in there. It's a place that's all his. Where he can do whatever he wants and say whatever he wants and, more importantly, eat and drink whatever he wants. And if there's a lawnmower lying there in fifty or sixty pieces with no hope of ever being re-assembled, well that's nobody's business. Compared to the intimidating environment of the house, with the designer furniture and the fancy drapes and the expensive carpets, the garage is pure comfort and relaxation. Sit anywhere in dirty clothes and put your feet up. You are the master of your environment, instead of vice versa. So, to the rest of the family, don't worry about Dad spending time out there in the garage. You know where he is. You know there's only so much trouble he can get into. He's there if you need him. And he will eventually come back into the house a much happier man.

How to Find Your True Age

I read about some guy on the Internet who has different ways of determining your true age. I think it's a formula based on your heart rate and blood pressure and weight and whatever. He himself is over 50 chronologically but is actually only 38.6 on this new measurement system. I think if you go to his website, you're already at least 40. Nobody young is concerned about their true age unless they get caught in a bar. But I've come up with other ways to measure a person's true age, with some amazing results:

- **Alcohol Intake**—Doctors say you should only take in one alcoholic drink per day. At that rate, my Uncle Ralph is 173 years old.

- **Hair Loss**—On average, men have experienced a 50% hair loss by the age of 40 and a 70% hair loss by the age of 65. By this measurement, boxing promoter Don King is 11.

- **Waist Measurement**—A person's girth increases by 2.5 cm. (1") every decade. This means I age by 15 years each Christmas.

- **Favorite TV Shows**—Since viewers relate best to people of their own generation, a person's true age is reflected in the TV shows they watch. If you watch South Park, your true age is 9. If you watch Baywatch, your true age is 36D. If you watch Lawrence Welk, you are reincarnated.

New Year's Revolutions

By now you've broken all your New Year's Resolutions and are feeling bad about it. Well don't. Just think how much worse shape you'd be in if you hadn't dieted for that whole week or quit drinking for that day. So don't beat yourself up for coming back to the same old you. The police and the medical community will tell you when it's time for you to change.

┌───┐
│   │
│   *Quote of the Day*   │
│   │
│   *"If you don't believe life is full of surprises,* │
│   *you've never changed a diaper."*   │
│   │
│   —*Red Green*   │
│   │
└───┘

Lower the Bar and Pull Up a Stool

When I was in high school my friends and I were exposed to a lot of hype from the guidance department on striving for excellence and being the best and always making sure that our reach exceeded our grasp. Frankly, that's created a lot of problems for all of us. Especially now that we're a little older and we've given up on excellence and being the best and many of us are down to our last grasp. The end result of forty-odd years of striving for unattainable goals is a deep sense of failure and ultimate worthlessness. This is not good. We need to reverse this trend by finding success in our lives. It's time to lower the bar. Here is a list of accomplishments that you can look at and say, "Hey. I'm a star!"

- You have some kind of a job and live in some kind of a dwelling.

- You have never spent more than a night or two in jail.

- At some point in your life, you've been able to get a loan.

- You've never killed anyone on purpose.

- You're not a quitter. You didn't quit those jobs—you were fired.

- You have never had an extramarital affair with a supermodel.

- When you go into a clothing store, you can still find one or two items that are too big for you.

- Although you've never been on A&E's Biography, you've also never been on America's Most Wanted.

- You have never done nearly as many stupid things as you've thought of.

- You don't whine.

Hitting Your Quota

If any of you have worked in a high-pressure sales organization, then you're familiar with the concept of having a quota of sales or contacts or whatever that you're expected to meet. I'm beginning to think that the quota system is a natural phenomenon that occurs in all aspects of human behavior. Yesterday I was trying to pull out of a side street. There were two cars approaching—the first was an elderly gentleman with his turn signal going and the second was a teenager with no signal on. The first car didn't turn but the second one did. What that shows me is that when we're young we don't use our turn signals and then when we get old we have to use them all the time because we need to meet our quota and we're running out of time. And it's true with lots of activities. People who sit quietly now probably did way too much talking in the past. And it's usually the same with non-smokers and non-drinkers. They used up their quota. Maybe even impotence is the ultimate acknowledgment of a job well done.

Make Sure You Worry Enough

I was watching an episode of Sixty Minutes last week and they had new evidence that life will eventually kill us. That show has been on the air for about a thousand years and I wonder how they've managed to come up with new things for us to worry about every week. I bet if they went back over their old shows, they'd find all kinds of catastrophes that just never happened. "Banking machines are dangerous" or "Ozone depletion will bring the end of life as we know it in the next four years" or "Disco music causes spinal damage." I notice that the worries are getting larger these days. Instead of uncovering corruption in Nicaragua, they're now telling us that our air is poisoned, our water supply is polluted, the polar caps are melting, and we have more garbage dumps than farms. I hate to sound irresponsible but I've lost the ability to get upset about these horrible problems. I just need somebody to tell me what to do and I'll gladly do it. I'll boil my water or stop dancing or store my garbage in rubber. Whatever it takes. Just don't tell me I should be worrying about things I can't understand or control. No wonder Seinfeld was a hit.

Getting Lucky

Looking back over the years, I notice how the phrase "getting lucky" has changed its meaning. When I was a little boy, "getting Lucky" meant retrieving my dog from the neighbor's patio party. After puberty, it took on a whole new implication. The teen years are in fact the golden era of getting lucky. Next, "getting lucky" referred to my first successful job application, then being approved for a mortgage, then surviving that tax audit, and then avoiding the axe during the company downsizing. Nowadays, "getting lucky" means the medical tests came back negative.

Quote of the Day

"Lawn ornaments are the handyman's way of getting back at the neighbors."

—*Red Green*

Going to the Dogs

They say that as people get older they really start to appreciate a pet. Like a dog. Some of the retirement homes bring dogs in on a regular basis as therapy for the residents. Apparently, once you have a few miles on you, you're ready to lower your standard of social interaction to the canine level. Personally, I don't understand the appeal of spending so much time and energy on something that can't talk to you. Or talk back to you. Or borrow your car without asking. Or use your money to flunk out of college. Or ruin its life and then blame you. But then maybe that's just me.

Quote of the Day

"If I knew then what I know now, I wouldn't have had any friends at all."

—*Red Green*

Watch Out for That Darned Computer

I use
a computer a
fair bit and, like
most people, I only
know enough about it
to make it do the things I need. And when it doesn't do what I
want, I try to trick it by trying oddball ways of doing the same
thing. Anything rather than read the manual or call the service
line and be put on hold for three hours of Kenny G.

And lately I'm really getting to resent my computer. It tells
me when I do an illegal operation. It beeps when it's not happy
with me. If I go on the Internet, it starts downloading material
that I never asked for. It won't even let me turn it off. It has all
the characteristics of a bad child, an abusive parent, and a loveless
marriage. I may have to go back to watching television.

Ten Ways to Maintain Your Privacy

If you're fed up with neighbors and strangers coming to your front door to visit or ask for your participation or to try to sell you something, here are some things to do that will keep them away:

- Place a "Watch for Land Mines" sign on your front lawn beside an exploded car.

- Keep a big dog chewing a pantleg on your porch.

- Rewire your doorbell so that it plays a tape of gun-shots.

- Cover your welcome mat with shards of broken beer bottles.

- Put one of those yellow "Police—Do Not Cross" tapes across the end of your driveway.

- On your front door hang a sign saying "Caution—Exorcism in Progress."

- Leave a pizza delivery car in your driveway with the door open and the engine running for a week or so.

- When you see someone approaching, start a chain-saw running inside the house.

- Place quarantine signs around your property.

- In the middle of the night, turn over a rectangle of your front lawn so that it looks like a fresh grave. Add another one every few months.

Working Too Hard Can Kill You

I hear about guys who work all their lives, saving up for their retirement, and then when they do finally get the golden handshake, they keel over in the first year. The most common theory is that men have a problem adjusting to suddenly having nothing to do and that the secret to a successful retirement is to keep busy, maintaining an active schedule and having real responsibilities. I don't agree. That sounds to me like you're supposed to solve the problem by making retirement more like work. I prefer to go the other way—make work more like retirement.

- Once you hit the age of forty, take one afternoon a week off work and go sit in the park.

- When you have a meeting, don't make any suggestions or comments, and when you're asked for an opinion, shrug it off.

- Come in late and leave early.

- Never answer your phone.

- Read novels at your desk.

- Avoid responsibility.

- You may take some flack, but when your retirement comes up, you'll be ready. And it may happen sooner than you expect.

How Far We Have Fallen

I read somewhere that after men pass the age of forty their body produces less testosterone. For most of us, this is a huge adjustment, as it represents the worst part of the aging process and, in some respects, a major career change. As with most setbacks in life, it's better to try to find some good news in there rather than to rail against the reality. (That's what saved my marriage.) So I've come up with a list of positive changes in your life, directly related to reduced levels of testosterone:

- When you talk to a woman wearing a tight sweater, you can now make eye contact.

- You're more informed because you watch the late news even though your wife is in bed. Awake.

- When you see a sexually explicit movie in the theater, you don't have to wait ten minutes before you can stand up.

- You watch PBS instead of Baywatch.

- Your wife can be affectionate without risk.

- More of your blood is going to your brain.

- You realize that your attractive secretary is actually pretty useless.

- You're getting a lot more sleep.

- When you go to a nudist colony, you'll be able to spot other men your age.

- There's always the chance of a pleasant surprise.

Grey Hair Means the End of Prime

I have a couple of friends my age who are appearing in big network television shows and they've each had to dye their hair to keep their jobs. Apparently, the television decision-makers don't think the audience can stand to see a grey-haired man on a prime-time series. Maybe it's because these decision-makers are 23 years old and they don't want men who look like their dads to be stars. But what a horrible message to those of us who have grey hair. Is it over for us? Will it come back with a bottle of Grecian formula?

For me, my face and hair are roughly the same age so they kind of go together. I don't think I'd look right with Ricky Martin's hair and he'd look just as bad with my face. When I look at myself in the mirror, I kind of think this is the way God wanted me to look—and if it's good enough for him, it's okay with me. However, God doesn't run the TV networks. That becomes more obvious every season.

Right-Sizing Your Home

A lot of people my age are making the move from a two-story, four-bedroom family home into a one-bedroom condo. They tell me that they want to reduce the maintenance work and general hassle of owning and maintaining a house, but I don't believe it. Sure, the condo management people will cut the lawn and shovel the snow and look after the outside maintenance, but they charge you a few hundred bucks a month to do it. Chances are you could have had the same level of service for the same price on your own house. Maintenance is not the issue—it's all about downsizing. Downsizing is not a new concept. Life does it to most of us. Haven't you ever noticed how much smaller your grandfather is than he used to be?

We've been battling life from our four-bedroom fort every day for a lot of years. Now that we're running out of ammo, we need to be a smaller target. Maybe in a condo with security, the world won't bother us as often. And of course, no extra room means no extra visitors. No matter who drops in, at some point it's going to get late and you're going to have to go to bed and they're going to have to go home. And you will have peace. That's what this is all about. Moving to a condo is you giving up on conquest and instead, opting for peace. You've always found peace in the smallest room in the home. Now you're hoping to find it in the smallest home on the block.

Conflicting Messages

Life is so much more difficult because of the conflicting messages that bombard us throughout our lives. And the frequency of these messages has a great impact on our decision making. If you get bad advice ten times more often than you get good advice, your chances of making the right decision are extremely remote. The behavioral recommendations I get in church on Sunday morning are in direct conflict with the ones from the bartender and his able-bodied assistants on Monday through Saturday. And church doesn't have a happy hour.

And you get the same ratio from TV commercials. For every one promoting diet and fitness, there are a hundred pushing burgers and fries. What chance do we have against these kinds of odds? Maybe that's what happens to the president. Maybe he's got one guy telling him to do the right thing and a hundred others advising him that it's business as usual. So here's an easy solution that we can all live by—listen to everybody's opinions, but take your own advice.

The Trunk Says It All

You can pretty much tell how old a driver is by examining the contents of his trunk:

- **Spare Tire**—Over 30

- **Spare Tire with air in it**—Over 50

- **Sleeping Bag**—Under 20

- **Sleeping Bag for sleeping**—Over 60

- **Laundry**—Single, over 20

- **Clean Laundry**—Recently separated, over 40

- **Snow shovel**—Over 30

- **Snowblower**—Over 50

- **Bag of sand**—Over 20

- **Bag of Viagra**—Over 70

- **Body Bag**—Over and Out.

The Rule of Thumb

I've been a husband for most of my adult life and certainly all of my mature adult life and I've watched the relationship evolve over that period of time. I find that the average married woman regards her husband as some strange life form who means well but basically doesn't get it. He becomes an obstacle to a quiet, easy, stress-free life. Someone who has to be cajoled and coaxed and tricked into doing things like shopping or having the relatives over. I'd just like to point out that the role of being the opposition is a valuable one that is reflected in court procedures and parliamentary government. Husbands are the opposing thumbs of relationships. There is an implied mutual dependency as the contrary positions of husband and wife make both parties stronger and more effective. Without husbands, the wives would simply be four fingers waving in the breeze, and without wives, husbands would just be a thumb, hitchhiking its way through life.

Cash 'n' Carry

There are many differences between men and women and all of them are at least interesting. Many are even mind-boggling. For example, women have no respect for pockets. Men live for them. A place to keep money, treasures, notes, car keys, your wallet, and your hands as a signal that you approach life as an uninvolved spectator. Women don't like pockets because they add bulk. Women are uncomfortable with bulk. The pocket adds two layers of material and, if you put something in the pocket, it's even worse. Women prefer to use a purse. It's not just the bulk thing. Women carry more equipment—make-up and hair devices and various personal items. No garment would ever have enough pockets. So, as odd as it may seem, I say we just leave well enough alone. Let the women stay with the purses. If they ever switch to pockets and then start standing around with their hands in them, that would only mean more work for us.

The Big Choice

Somebody told me that Sigmund Freud said people have to make a choice between love and work. To me that sounds like a man who hates his job, but apparently what he meant was that you focus your efforts on love (connecting with your life partner, your family, your friends, your community) or work (being competent, successful, respected in your industry). So naturally, I've tried to figure out which one I am. I decided that I focus my efforts on work. Except every couple of months that goes down the dumper, so then I focus on family and friends until they bug the living daylights out of me and I go back to work. According to Freud, that means I resented my father. Now I also resent Freud.

Quote of the Day

"The Internet has it all wrong. Men my age don't want to be interactive. We don't even want to be active."

—*Red Green*

A Bridge Too Far

It's funny how you can get so confused in your life that your ability to make judgments becomes seriously impaired. I've been going through some financial challenges lately, as well as a few extended-family speed bumps, and it's affected my opinion of those guys who live under the bridge. To have no job pressures, no mortgage payments, no expectation from yourself or others, no cell phone, no sales pressure, no wardrobe choices—it doesn't look that bad to me. But like I say, I'm confused.

Quote of the Day

"Opinions are like toothbrushes. Everybody has one so there's no need to share."

—Red Green

Location, Location, Location

My whole life can be traced by what I wanted to live close to. As a kid, I wanted to live close to the playground. Then I wanted to live close to the friends that I made at the playground. Then my girlfriend. Then the tavern. Then my job. Then the school. Then the golf course. Then the doctor's office. Now the hospital. And finally, the funeral home. (I'm counting on a big turnout.)

Ten Expressions That Give Away Your Age

- Groovy.

- Lucky Strike Means Fine Tobacco.

- You got it, Pontiac!

- Far out.

- Avon calling.

- Make my day.

- Book 'em, Dano.

- To the moon, Alice.

- What's your sign?

- I think the president is telling the truth.

Quote of the Day

"In my life, the only things that have gone up in value are love, friendship and sleep."

—*Red Green*

If Looks Could Kill

Now that I've got a lot more white hair in my beard and a lot less of any-colored hair on my head, I can't help but notice how people look at me differently. I know what they're doing. They're pigeonholing me. Stereotyping me. Classifying me as a burnt-out old guy who should be dead soon. Maybe I'm over-sensitive, but I resent that. I had a guy tailgating me because I was going pretty slow in the passing lane. I like the passing lane. No ramps. No trucks. And I'm closer to oncoming traffic, which helps keep me awake. Finally, this guy swings around and passes me on the right, and he looks over at me to express some type of four-letter critique of my driving, but then he sees my old face and makes a gesture that implies, "I should have known it would be an old guy." That bugged me, so here's what I decided. Think of your self-image as a flashlight. Think of other people's opinion of you as another flashlight. If their flashlight is brighter than yours, you have a problem. I'm working hard to make sure that doesn't happen to me. I hope I don't run out of batteries.

I Think, Therefore I Am Woman

My wife and I had a little disagreement the other night and I was sitting out in the garage trying to figure out where we went wrong. I decided it was during the Industrial Revolution. Up until then, men and women were on a pretty equal footing. Men worked in the fields while women worked in the home. After the big I.R., the women still worked in the home but the men were now working in mines and factories. This was a huge setback. When you're working in the fields or the home, you can think about things. Doing the laundry or bringing in the sheaves are jobs that don't require much of your mind, so you can be postulating theories or examining relationships while you're working. But when you're setting off a dynamite charge or working with a 200-ton punch press, you'd better give it your full attention. That's why during the Industrial Revolution, men stopped thinking. At first it was just a work thing so that they could keep their fingers. But eventually it permeated all phases of men's lives. Meanwhile women just kept thinking and thinking. And by the time we hit the twentieth century where they started working every bit as much as men, the women had been thinking for so long that they couldn't stop—whereas with men the exact opposite was true.

Make Sure You're Caught Napping

We have a thirteen-year-old dog who doesn't look or listen as well as he used to, but otherwise seems just fine. They tell me he's ninety-one in human years, and I'd say he's got another thirty or so to go. I've been studying him to discover his secrets to longevity, hoping I could apply them to my life. I ruled out drinking from the toilet bowl, and my wife kiboshed relieving myself on the lawn. That left the naps. My dog has about seven naps a day. That's a dog day. That equates to seven human days. In other words, to a dog, the time between naps is a day. What a great concept. That's something I should do. If I have four naps a day and count each space in between as a day, it will completely change my life. Sure, it'll screw up my calendar, but I'll be well rested, and I'll live to be a hundred and sixty.

Quote of the Day

"If information was medicine, most of it would be a laxative."

—Red Green

Old Friends Save Time

When I was younger, I would make friends easily and drop them the same way. I was easygoing then. Not so judgmental. And anybody who says otherwise is a moron. But now that I'm a little more experienced, or "previously enjoyed," as the luxury used-car salesmen say, I've changed my whole approach towards friends. At my age, I don't want to make new friends. I want to keep the old ones. With the old ones, I don't have to waste precious time explaining things. Like how I got that scar or why I'm not allowed to cross the border. In Hollywood, they call it backstory. I don't have the time or energy to go through my backstory. I want to be with friends who already know it and are sick of hearing about it and who would rather pretend to have forgiven me for it than to force me to bring it up. And I know a few embarrassing things about them, too, so it's a level playing field. My advice is, if you have old friends, stick with them. They are a great source of comfort for the rest of the trip. And the fact that somebody who has known you for a long period of time still finds you tolerable is a great compliment and flies in the face of many of your wife's theories.

Where the Boys Are

There seems to be a rash of young female pop singers these days. And I mean real young. Like, say, twelve or thirteen. But they look a lot older, and they have all the gyrations of a potential arrest. And now we have a whole generation of eleven-year-old girls who are emulating these young stars by wearing make-up and revealing clothes and so on. I'm thinking this has to make life very difficult for eleven-year-old boys. Not only are the girls a foot taller and a lot smarter, but they also look like your much older sister. And you know how she treats you. This is a terrible hardship for today's eleven-year-old boys. It's almost like the lucky ones are gay.

Keep Looking Forward

There is a tendency as we get older to spend too much time looking back. It's natural. At this age, your life is like looking at yourself naked in a mirror—the biggest part is behind you. A little reminiscing is okay, but you're better off to stay focused on the future—and the shorter it is, the more attention you should pay to it. The trick is to stay optimistic about the future, so here's a list of things you can look forward to in your declining years:

- Nobody's going to ask you to help them move.

- Friends will stop trying to set you up with their sisters.

- Life insurance salesmen will stop calling.

- Product warranties will become less of a concern.

- You can have a young woman live with you, and people will assume she's a nurse.

- You can stop trying to lose weight.

- You can be the center of attention by always taking your will to family gatherings.

Being Good at What You Enjoy Being Good At

My wife was talking about a friend of ours, commenting on how successful he'd been. We've been married long enough for me not to take that as a criticism, no matter how it was intended. I did say that this guy really enjoys his job, and my wife answered, "That's why he's good at it." I've heard that before, and I still don't agree with it. It's based on a fallacy. You're not good at something just because you enjoy it. Karaoke has proven that.

To my way of thinking, you're not good at something because you enjoy it; rather, you enjoy something because you're good at it. And you need to have proof that you're good at it. People have complimented you, or you've won awards or been promoted. If you continue to do things without getting that kind of feedback, then your enjoyment is inversely proportional to someone else's suffering. You're not good at it. You're just at it. And the reason you enjoy it is because you're oblivious to the fact that others are allowing you to do it because of stringent societal regulations concerning assault and homicide. So, in the future, please make sure you're good at something before you start to enjoy it. If we all do that, there'll be an instant upgrade in party jokes, after-dinner speeches, and honeymoons.

So Much Choice, So Little Time

One thing that experience tells a person is that things are rarely what they seem. From the actual take-home amount of that first paycheck to your first personal encounter involving nudity, there are always disappointments and compromises that must be made on a mutual basis. I've also been shocked to learn that although having no choice in life is a bad thing, and having some choice in life is a good thing, having lots of choice in life is a horrible thing. Think of your life decisions as movies in a video store. You want to pick from maybe five alternatives—drama, action, comedy, classic or even a musical if you have no minimum level. You don't want to be faced with the thousand options they have staring at you. Instead of being able to make a decision and move forward, you'll spend your life looking at the choices and eating free popcorn. Too much choice is a bad thing. That's why ugly people do better in a small town.

Quote of the Day

"Ideas are like children. In most cases, the conception is the only fun part."

—Red Green

Signs That You Are Too Old to Have Children

Don't let fertility fool you. Just because you're still capable of producing offspring, that doesn't mean you should. Here are the signs that it's time to hang up your guns:

- You hate all noise that you're not making.

- You don't want to explain anything.

- You think that the next diaper that comes into your life should be yours.

- A mid-life crisis and a minivan are not mutually compatible.

- You don't want to spend any part of your golden years at a parent-teacher meeting.

- None of the rooms in your home would look better with Fisher-Price accents.

- Whatever strength is left in your back, you're reserving for beer cases.

- From here on out, you want to be the center of attention.

The Living Will

Breakthroughs in medical science are wreaking havoc on the tradition of having each generation benefit from the toils of the former one. In the old days, when mid-forties was the life expectancy, a man would pass away and leave his estate or his farm or his blacksmith tools or whatever to his son, who would be in his early twenties and could really use that stuff. Now we've got people living for eighty years and more, and it'll only get worse. I think we'll see the time when it will be common for people to live past the age of one hundred. That'll really mess things up. What is the point of dying at the age of a hundred and ten and leaving everything to your ninety year-old son? It's a little late. So you might think about leaving it to your grandson who's only seventy. Or your great-grandson who's fifty. But to really make a difference in someone's life they have to get it much earlier. So you'd end up leaving everything to your great-great-great-grandchildren who are barely blood relatives and virtual strangers. So I say your best bet is to spend the money before you die and spend it on somebody you know really well—yourself. If my wife is reading this, that boat I've been looking at is still for sale.

Last Call

The other day I saw a guy walking through the park with his sweetheart. They were holding hands and strolling in a leisurely fashion like the people in those French movies do. And the whole time, he's talking to somebody on his cell phone. Nothing urgent. Just talking leisurely to an acquaintance while he meanders through the trees with his significant other. Now, I'm not a relationship expert, but when your partner would rather make small talk over the phone than talk to you, I think it's time to hang that one up. And make sure you reverse the charges.

Quote of the Day

"Simple things last forever. Just look at my grandfather."

—*Red Green*

Getting Short with Tall Guys

I'm not a tall person. Just barely average height, actually. So I've always had tall guys around me, taking charge, attracting women, helping me find my car in a crowded parking lot, that kind of thing. I always feel somehow disadvantaged around tall guys, so I'd like to use this space for a little "get even" time. I know the tall guys won't listen, but maybe you normal people will.

First of all, tall guys are here to mate with tall women and have tall children to ensure the future of the NBA. A short guy going out with a tall girl takes a special kind of man who is very well-adjusted and doesn't have a bald spot. Short guys want to go out with short girls. Short girls are hard to find, and short attractive girls are a small percentage of that group. So when a tall guy starts dating an attractive short girl, all of the Laws of Nature are at risk. Tall guys should not be allowed to go out with short girls. They should have a sign on their tie saying, "You must be this tall to go on this ride."

And don't be fooled, ladies. Just because a guy is tall doesn't mean he's smart. His brain has a lot of heavy work to do—moving that huge body around without falling over, ducking under doorways, and avoiding lightning. A short guy's brain can think about other things—like you. Short guys make better lovers. They're more responsive, more attentive, and more grateful. And they won't get in your way personally or professionally. With a short guy, you can have your ear to the ground and still maintain eye contact.

E is for Enough

I know I've been somewhat critical of technology from time to time, but when it comes to e-mail, all is forgiven. E-mail is the greatest form of communication since the wink. It's quick, it's effortless, it's free, and you don't have to lick anything. There is no better way to contact people or even call your mother. For one thing, it's undaunting. It's a small space you have to fill. By the time you say hello and mention the weather and your bursitis, you only have room to say goodbye. And it's the best part of communication—the transmitting part. Not the receiving part. It's every man's dream—a one-way conversation. Oh sure, people can e-mail you back, but you can delete that without reading it. Is this a great thing or what? If any of you disagree with this, please send me your comments. My e-mail address is likeIcare@I'llgetrightonthat.com.

The Longest Drive

We have laws in this country that once you reach the age of 80, you have to have a driver's test every year. A lot of men dread it because they know that'll be the end of their driving career. The truth is, most driving careers should end long before they get that far. I see middle-aged people in restaurants who don't see well enough to read the menu or the wine list or the bill, let alone hop into their cars and drive home. Right now the cops pull you over for spot checks to catch drunk drivers and unsafe vehicles, but if the program was expanded to include surprise driving tests, a lot of us would be walking home. Now I'm not saying you 80-year-olds are being picked on. I agree you don't drive any worse than the rest of us, but you've been getting away with it for a lot longer. So stop dreading the driver's test when you turn 80. It may give you your best chance to reach 81.

Quote of the Day

"My friend spent so much time in the donut shop that he was arrested for impersonating a police officer."

—Red Green

Garbage In, Garbage Out

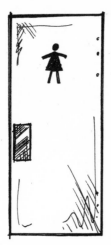

I'm not sure exactly when I figured out that people are made up of chemicals, but my guess would be sometime in the '60s. We are all complex mixtures of the various chemicals that make up our beings. A change in the chemicals makes a change in the person. Hydrogen and oxygen make water. That's it. Anything you add makes a huge difference. You can't also throw in a boatload of Bunker C Crude and still have water, as everyone at Exxon now knows. So we should all be aware of the chemicals we are putting into our bodies on a daily basis. The more chemicals, the more chemical reactions. The more chemical reactions, the less chance of you making new friends or being allowed back into the hot tub. You'll need to do a lot of your own research on this because everyone's different, but as a general rule, never mix carbonated over-proof alcoholic fruit drinks with any type of cheese derivative having a pH above 9.

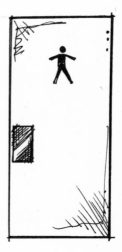

The Not-So-Sweet Smell of Success

Okay, here's the thing that's bad about successful people. They tend to be successful in most things. If they're good at running a successful business, they're probably good at running a successful family too. That's fine, and congratulations to them, but the last thing you need is to spend time with a person who not only makes ten times your annual salary but also gets along better with his kids. And no matter how much you think you get along with that successful guy, somewhere deep down inside, each of you is thinking, "What a dink."

Quote of the Day

"It's very humbling when the voices in your head are talking to somebody else."

—*Red Green*

(L-R) RED GREEN (Steve Smith), MIKE HAMAR (Wayne Robson), HAROLD GREEN (Patrick McKenna) and the rest of the Possum Lodge gang try to find humor in being sued by a local businessman in RED GREEN'S DUCT TAPE FOREVER.

RED GREEN (Steve Smith) stands before the court.

HAROLD GREEN (Patrick McKenna) and RED GREEN (Steve Smith) address the Possum Lodge

EDGAR MONTROSE (Graham Greene) shows RED GREEN (Steve Smith) his explosive solution to every problem.

The Possum Lodge gang lends a hand when Robert Stiles' limousine falls into a sink hole.

(L-R) DEPUTY DAWN (Melissa DiMarco) corners HAROLD GREEN (Patrick McKenna) after he siphons gas out of her police vehicle.

(L-R) RED GREEN (Steve Smith) and his nephew, HAROLD GREEN (Patrick McKenna) soon discover that the bitter Sheriff will stop at nothing to make sure they don't arrive at the Duct Tape contest.

After being towed behind the van and chased for days, the Possum Lodge's giant duct tape goose arrives at the Annual Duct Tape contest.

Passion erupts between DEPUTY DAWN (Melissa DiMarco) and HAROLD GREEN (Patrick McKenna) after Harold is awarded an official Possum Lodge vest for bravery in RED GREEN'S DUCT TAPE FOREVER.

Things You Can Say Now

As the years go by, there's an unwritten law allowing you privileges that you've never had before. While you may not be able to do as many things as you used to, you can now say more stuff than you ever could. Here is a list of expressions that are only acceptable once you hit mid-life and beyond:

- These days, there's too much sex in everything. Except my life.

- Tell the waiter to bring me something soft.

- You're both sitting in my chair.

- We were the first family on our street to have a television.

- We were the first family on our street to have a radio.

- We were the first family on our street.

Ten Indicators Your Company Is About to Downsize

- During the lunch break, nobody can find the want ads because your boss has them.

- Your company just had a bad year. Or a good year. Or an average year.

- The company president traded in his BMW for a Hyundai.

- Extra boxes of Kleenex are brought in for the directors' meeting.

- The company replaces the nurse with someone named Kevorkian.

- Your office is being used to store Star Wars merchandise.

- Your boss tells the courier about your excellent work habits and asks, "Are they hiring?"

- Your request for a pay increase is met with stunned silence, then laughter.

- Everyone in senior management is spending most of the day in the restroom.

- You have shareholders.

Too Close to Call

So, I was at a mall and I had locked the keys in my car and I was trying to phone a locksmith. I walked up to the pay phone and grabbed the phone book to look up a locksmith's number.

Here's where the trouble starts. Not only does the phone book have a font the size of ant droppings, it is also on a very short leash. Too short for me to be able to get it close enough to my face to read it. Why do they do that? And I can't phone information because I don't know the name of any locksmiths. So I'm forced to bend over in a public place.

I don't know whether it was my back cramping up or the laughter of the teenage girls or the fact that a neighbor recognized me from that angle, but as I rode home on the bus I vowed never to use a pay phone again.

The Last Shall Be First

I need some computer nerd out there to come up with software that will allow me to scan a contract into my computer, and then enlarge the fine print and put it at the top of the document. That would save me a lot of eyestrain and a lot of ink. When my wife said, "Why do they make the important things so small?" I said it was just Nature's way.

Quote of the Day

"If it looks like a duck and walks like a duck, it's probably about my age."

—Red Green

Some Assembly Required

My wife bought a computer desk this week in the form of two boxes sticking out of the car trunk, each of which outweighed me. I wrestled them into the living room and tried to open the boxes carefully, but I'm not at my best when something heavy has just fallen on my foot. Inside were a couple of dozen slabs of fake wood, five bags of hardware, and a twenty-seven-page instruction manual. I learned to read instruction manuals last summer after I assembled a five-speed bicycle and it turned out to be a wheelbarrow. Three days and a bunch of repeated steps later, the desk was together. So now I'm thinking, "What if we don't like it and want to take it back?" I've already scratched it and wrecked the box, and I'd have to take it apart just to get it into the car. And it struck me that unassembled furniture is like a marriage. It may not be perfect, but when you consider the hassle of taking it back, you stick it in the corner and try not to look at it too closely. And everyone knows you made it yourself.

A Must to Avoid

You've taken steps so that you won't be reminded that you're getting older. You avoid mirrors and brightly lit rooms and anyone who knows your true age, but there are physical activities that you should also stay away from. If you want to maintain that healthy young self-image, pay attention to the following:

- If you drop something, don't bend over. If you can't pick it up with your toes, write it off.

- Don't run. People will forgive your tardiness much more readily than your red face, your heavy breathing, or the fact that your stomach is still bouncing.

- Don't get into any vehicle that's short enough for you to see over. You may never get out.

- Don't wear tight clothing or stand in the wind. Keep your shape a mystery.

- Don't dance. You don't know any modern steps, you can't hear the music all that well, and songs are a lot longer than they used to be.

Together Again

I saw another one of those long-lost-brother reunion things on one of those talk shows for people who tell their whole family to shut up so they can watch a television program on communicating. On this particular episode, a brother and sister were brought back together after twenty years of no contact. Now, it was a touching scene when they hugged each other and shed a tear or two, but I had a sense that this was all a huge invasion of privacy. We've got the Internet and the phone book and there are only six degrees of separation, so I have to believe that any two people that want to find each other, do. When you see a reunion, that means the person who wanted to do the finding did a way better job than the person who wanted to do the hiding. It looks good for a few minutes on television, but an hour later I'll bet somebody says, "By the way, you still owe me money or an apology or both." So if there's anybody out there trying to reunite with somebody, you can't find the person because they don't want to meet you halfway, and there's probably a good reason for that. Focus instead on the people who've been with you all the way along. Unless you owe them money. Or an apology. Or both.

Those Wacky Kids

I was talking to some friends whose son just did something really stupid. To me that just proves he's not adopted, but they're upset about it. Now I know there are serious problems that children can get into as they're growing up, but I think that mistakes and harmless goofy things are very important. It's a great learning experience for them and it's also a comfort for a parent to know they're not the only goofball in the family. Yes, you want your kids to be successful, but not too successful. It's embarrassing to have a brilliant kid or a son who's a millionaire. It makes you look like a loser because you couldn't do what he did. Or worse yet, it implies that your wife's genes are the ones responsible for your son's success.

Quote of the Day

"Television shows that make you think are almost as bad as reading a book."

—Red Green

Who Is King of the Jungle?

We all know we need to save the planet and protect the animals and all that stuff, but once in a while we need to remind ourselves of the various priority levels occupied by plant and animal life. Here are a few signs that something is out of whack with Nature's pecking order:

- The dog has eaten your lunch.

- You're sleeping on the couch because the cat is on your pillow.

- You can't take a vacation because you can't find anyone to feed the fish.

- The Parks Department is fining you because you allowed a tree to fall on your home.

- You saved so much heating fuel last winter that you contracted pneumonia in the comfort of your own family room.

- You can't go out to a friend's house because your kids have the car.

Stick with Your Own Generation

My nephew was complaining to me the other day about his part time job at a fast food place where he works indoors wearing a uniform for $5.80 an hour and all the saturated fat he can stuff into his fanny pack. I was telling him about when I was a kid working as a milkman's helper out in the freezing cold for a two-dollar bill a day. He had no idea what I was talking about. He'd never heard of a milkman or seen a two-dollar bill. I'm not even sure he knows what freezing cold is. And I didn't try to educate him because I've been married long enough to know that most things can't be explained. The person either gets it or they don't. And it's not their fault. My nephew has just as much trouble trying to tell me what he's learning in school or why he likes that music or how much more hardware he's planning to attach to his facial features. The message is that we should all hang out with our own peer groups. The people of our generation have a lot more chance of understanding what we're talking about and forgiving us for what we've done. I recommend that you marry someone who's around your age, work for a boss from your own era, and always give your side of the story to the cop with the gray hair.

The Call Waiting Is the Hardest Part

I was talking to an acquaintance on the phone the other day and I heard that telltale break-up in their voice that indicates another phone call coming in on call waiting. They ignored it. And then I remembered all of the other times I'd been talking to people and the second they would get another call, they would say, "Hang on a minute. I'm getting another call," and would leave me to go get it. So now I've decided that another person's response to their call waiting is a pretty good indication of your relationship. If they refuse to take the other call no matter what, you're solid. If they wait until the other call interrupts several times or they tell you they're expecting an important call and then excuse themselves, that's still okay. But if they jump at the first chance to bail out of talking to you, well that can only mean that you have no—Hang on a minute. I'm getting another call.

Laughter Is Not Always the Best Medicine

A preliminary list of bad times to laugh:

- When you're meeting your new boss.

- When the judge asks if you'd been drinking.

- The first time you see your girlfriend in a bathing suit.

- When the auditor asks if you declared your full income.

- When someone you're hoping to inherit money from drops their teeth.

- When you've just been threatened by a motorcycle gang.

- When someone you're married to stubs their toe.

- Anytime in church or anywhere that nobody else is laughing.

Stomaching Each Other

I've been married over 30 years, and when people ask me how you can make a relationship last that long, I tell them you have to marry the right person. I compare it to food. Now, sure, you may like spicy food once in a while, but over the long haul, you're better off with meat and potatoes. Something that will sustain you over the years without destroying your body. You need to pick a meat-and-potatoes type of partner. And don't think you can sneak out once in a while for a spicy snack. Your wife can always tell.

Quote of the Day

"Love is blind. Marriage is an eye-opener."

—*Red Green*

Ways to Make Your Neighbors Think You're Rich

Perception is everything. Here are a few ways to make your neighbors think you're rich:

- Once a week arrive home honking the horn, jump out of the car, and pop a champagne cork, then rush inside laughing. (Quickly re-insert the cork so you're ready for next week.)

- Have a set of magnetic signs that you stick on the sides of any trucks parked in front of your house: Excelsior Indoor Pools, Monarch Billiard Tables, Deluxe Home Theater.

- Once a month come out of your house with your briefcase handcuffed to your wrist. Look around furtively while your son, dressed as a policeman, escorts you to your car. Speed off.

- Stop at a fancy restaurant and pick up their empty expensive wine bottles for you to put out in your recycling box.

- Make a deal with a friend whereby you cut each other's lawns.

Give Me the Big House

They say that as you get older and the kids move out, you're supposed to downsize your house. I don't want to do that. As I age, I want more space, not less. My coordination will be down a notch or two and I'll probably have a few more pounds on me, so I need generous doorways with lots of clearance. And I won't be getting out as much as I do now, so the house will be my whole world. I don't want to live in a world where I can see all four of its corners from anywhere in the living room. And when you're living in one open room, you have to put your projects away all the time, as well as explain the paint stains and the burn marks to people who don't understand the handyman mindset. Give me a big house with lots of rooms for my twilight years. Those tiny retirement homes aren't for me. I may think small, but I live big.

The Sliding Scale

I sometimes find it amazing that we all have such differing opinions about each other. I think it's because we pay so much attention to ourselves. We look in the mirror a lot, we think about things, we try to figure out problems, we often listen to what we have to say much more intently, because we consider our comments to be the highlight of the conversation. We are very familiar with ourselves physically, mentally, and spiritually, so we each become the measuring device by which we judge the world around us. So when we say someone is smart or attractive, we really mean "by comparison." For example, I think Regis Philbin is a pretty smart guy, but would Albert Einstein feel the same way about him? Of course, the corollary to this theory is that you're going to be judged the same way. You will only seem smart to people who are dumber than you, and you will only seem attractive to people who are uglier than you. You might want to keep that in mind when you're looking for friends or soul mates. Now, occasionally you see an exception, like in my case where you find an ugly guy married to a beautiful woman. But that's not Science, that's Love. Or Martyrdom.

Bring Back the Gold Star

Back when I was in elementary school, we had a point system whereby a student could accumulate points over the week and have a shot at going home on Friday with a gold star. I miss that. We need to bring that sense of success back into our lives. Here's a sample list of achievable rewards. Get a hundred points and the gold star is yours:

Went to work most days ✔ 10 pts.

Vacuumed potato chip fallout around Lazy Boy ✔ 15 pts.

Bought flowers for your wife ✔ 20 pts.

Bought flowers for somebody else's wife ✔ -20 pts.

Said "no" to something illegal, immoral, or fattening ✔ 10 pts.

Watched a half-hour of PBS ✔ 10 pts.

Looked at your wife when she was talking to you ✔ 15 pts.

Listened to your wife when she was talking to you ✔ 25 pts.

Loaned money to your adult son ✔ 20 pts.

Got money back from your adult son ✔ 0 pts. (unnecessary)

Had an ache and didn't mention it ✔ 15 pts.

Had a surprise for your wife ✔ 10 pts.

Had a pleasant surprise for your wife ✔ 50 pts.

The Bigger the Batter

Watching your weight is so much easier when you're young and are trying to attract members of the opposite sex, or any sex, but even after you get married and are encouraged to give up attracting admirers, it's important not to get carried away. It's very easy to put on a couple of pounds a year, but after fifty years, that's an extra hundred pounds. You not only need bigger clothes, you need a bigger car which means a bigger garage which usually means a bigger house, all of which means bigger payments, which will add bigger stress and lead you to an earlier and bigger grave, occupied by a bigger and more expensive coffin. So the next time you're ordering lunch at your favorite gourmet restaurant, remember that the phrase "Large size it" can do the same thing to your body and your bills.

It's Not How Good You Look, It's How Hard You Try

As we get a little older and lose the blush of youth, and the slimness of youth and the smoothness of youth and the hair of youth and the youngness of youth, we need to recalibrate our instruments when evaluating our level of attractiveness. For most of us over forty and beyond, it's not fair to be judged on whether or not we look good. How can we possibly look good? We didn't look good in our prime and we haven't appreciated over time. Instead, we now need to be judged on how much effort we put into our appearance. Did we shower? Put on fresh clothes? Shave? Get a haircut? Do we smell nice? Women love that. There's something inspirational about a person who keeps fighting insurmountable odds. You've seen the photos, you've looked in the mirror and yet you keep trying. Your partner will recognize these initiatives as attempts to please and will reward you. Maybe not with style points, but certainly with effort points—and at our age that and Miss Congeniality may be all there is.

Good Signs of Bad Feelings

It's always good to know where you stand with people, but many of us have difficulty communicating with clarity. So here are a few signs that will indicate that someone really doesn't like you:

- They refuse to make eye contact. Even when you're standing on their foot.

- They try to sell you Amway stuff.

- When you ask them to drive you home from work, they claim they brought the unicycle that day.

- When you talk to them, they look like they're having a really big cramp of some kind.

- When they see you're the only elevator passenger, they wait for the next one.

- They suggest you run for political office.

The Art of Stifling

Not that there's ever a good time to yawn, but we middle-aged married men are frequently facing really really bad times to yawn. These almost always involve a spouse who's upset about something we've said or done. We know they're right and we feel true remorse, but yawns happen. Especially after say 8 p.m. Nothing good will happen if you yawn while you're having behavior modification. You need to learn how to hide a yawn. I suggest you stand in front of a mirror and practice clenching your teeth really hard but without showing any movement of facial muscles. This may require weight gain but you should do whatever you have to. Try turning a yawn into a cough. Sometimes that works. Just make sure your mouth is relatively empty. As a last resort, go with the "lookaway" where you turn your head at least 97 degrees and run to the window. When she asks what's wrong, hold up your hand to buy enough time to complete the yawn and then say you thought you saw a robin or an alien spacecraft or something. Of course, the best policy is to make your faux pas early enough in the day so that the whole discussion takes place well before the Yawning Hour.

The Commitments

I met a guy last week who is very socially active. He's involved with this and that and the other and he doesn't seem to get much out of any of them. That's because he's involved in so many things, he doesn't have time to be committed to any one of them. There's a big difference between being involved and being committed. Like with bacon and eggs: the chicken is involved, the pig is committed. You must make a commitment. Marriage is the most popular one, but there are others—spending two months' salary on golf clubs, feeding a stray cat, getting your football team's logo tattooed on your forehead, buying the first round, being the first one in the hot tub to remove their bathing suit (unless you're alone or immediately become that way). So if you're not getting enough out of life, don't do more—do less, but do it harder.

A Change Will Do You Good

Acceptance is a key component for a happy life. Chances are your physiology has evolved considerably throughout your adult life. Your senses are somewhat less sharp, your patience and perseverance have diminished, and your annual weight increase has outperformed the stock market. All of these factors affect your wardrobe.

Do not wear the following:

- Shoes with laces.

- Tight jeans and t-shirts or any other clothes that have nowhere to keep your reading glasses.

- Anything stretchy or see-through.

- Anything that says Bay City Rollers on it.

- Anything with buttons smaller than an Oreo.

- Anything sleeveless.

- Anything with a plunging neckline.

- Shorts.

Are You Up for It?

There is a peculiar disease that has plagued the men in my family. In fact, it seems to apply to almost all men in all families. I think it's called Riser's Syndrome. There's only one easy-to-spot symptom—as you get into middle age and beyond, you find yourself getting up earlier and earlier. A man who used to sleep till lunch at 27 will leap out of bed at the crack of dawn at 48. And the disease seems to progress as you get older. Generally you get up an hour earlier for every ten years of your age. So at 30, if you were getting up at 7, at 40 you'll get up at 6, at 50 you'll get up at 5, and so on. If you live long enough, you actually run the risk of getting up before you go to bed.

That's why older men start back-timing their bedtimes. We yawn through dinner, nap on the couch, and generally try to hit the sack by 9:30 p.m. This can be very inconvenient for our wives and family, not to mention our dinner guests. So I've come up with a solution. If you're going to bed at 9 and getting up at 5, you're getting 8 hours sleep—they're just not the right 8 hours. You need to move east—two time zones east—where 9 p.m. becomes 11 p.m. and 5 a.m. becomes 7 a.m. That's acceptable for anybody. And in another ten years, you'll have to move farther and farther east. Keep doing this and you will always be keeping proper hours, no matter how old you get. Besides, I hear China is a great place to live.

The Golden Handshake

These days a lot of guys are being offered an early retirement package. And most of them are taking it. Mainly because their feelings are hurt by a company that, after twenty-five years of service, says, "You are so useless we're offering you a bonus to quit." I know this can be a difficult time, but before you take an early retirement of any kind, there are a few people you should check with. First, your wife. Is she going to let you mope around in your pajamas watching Oprah, or is she expecting the laundry done and dinner on the table when she gets home from work? How do your kids feel about Dad lying on the couch while they're at school? What happens on Career Day when you come in with a crossword puzzle? How about the City Parks Department? Do they think their image as a thriving community will be enhanced by your presence on a bench somewhere? Don't do it. When they offer the early retirement, hold out for a big payday and a transfer to somewhere exotic. If you're useless enough, they might just go for it—and if you're not, they'll keep you.

Little Things Mean a Lot

I don't think it's reasonable to expect people to have a significant impact on the world and I don't think we should feel like failures when we don't. It's often the little things, the small accomplishments, the minor victories, that are the most satisfying. So for the sake of your own mental health, take a few minutes at the end of each day and try to focus on some simple tiny breakthrough that you had in the last 24 hours. Maybe you feel good about not eating that doughnut. Maybe you feel good about eating them all. It doesn't matter what it is. Look for small accomplishments. I consider every day when the police don't have to come to my home as a true blessing. Find ways to feel good about yourself. We can't all be Nelson Mandela or Albert Einstein or Jerry Springer.

Quote of the Day

"I went to Scotland in April and I'm pleased to report that world-wide drought and global warming are merely rumours."

—*Red Green*

The Joys of a Job You Don't Need

Life is like a car—there's only one driver's seat. And you want to be in that driver's seat as often as possible. Most of us get a shot at the driver's seat when we get older. After we've retired and have done all of our major spending and have set up enough of a pension to support ourselves. That's the ideal time to get a job. It can be any job, but it's better if you deal with the public, like, say, in a store or a post office or something. Because the beauty of this job is that you don't need it. You can conduct yourself in any way you feel is appropriate. Be rude to people. Ignore them. See how mad you can make them. Use this job as your way of getting back at all of the stupid clerks and officials you've had to put up with your whole life. You'll get rid of all your frustrations (actually, you're just passing them on). You'll get up anxious to go to work and you'll come home refreshed and energized. Being cantankerous will extend your life. Sure, you'll eventually be fired—but they'll have to pay you severance, and then you can go get a job that you need even less.

Never Stop Learning

Sometimes, at our age, we lose our enthusiasm for new experiences because we think we've tried everything or we've lost our confidence or we're tired of standing in line in the emergency ward. The trick is to pick out something you've never done that you can actually do. Friends and family may have suggestions. Maybe fly fishing or lawn bowling or origami. My wife suggested I try "not interrupting her," but that only led to an ongoing argument we have about time and space.

Quote of the Day

"Doctors are wrong. Numbness is not necessarily a bad thing."

—*Red Green*

Throw Out Old Information

   Once a year you really need to clean out your drawers. More
importantly, you have to throw out all of your old day planners.
They'll just make you feel stupid and old. I was thumbing
through a few of mine that I found in the back of my desk. They
go back a few years and they had some interesting entries:
March 12, 1965: "Cancel VHS machine. Order Beta instead."—
April 14, 1975: "Blow off meeting with Bill Gates"—February
4, 1997: "Buy Bre-X stock." Get rid of them all now so that you
can get on with your life. The secret to happiness in old age is to
erase all traces of personal blunders and let fading memory work
its magic. It's called the Nixon Approach.

Marriage—The Taxpayer's Revenge

I was at my accountant's recently and he was telling me that when a husband or wife passes on, there's no tax to be paid as long as they leave their entire estate to their spouse. Then when that surviving spouse passes on, all taxes become due and payable. Suddenly a light bulb went off in my head. If the surviving spouse re-marries immediately and then leaves everything to that person, the tax benefits continue. And if that new person is a lot younger than the surviving spouse, the benefits go on for a long long time. Now I know why you'll often see an old guy with a really young second wife. That ain't no lady, that's a tax shelter.

Quote of the Day

"Always think of yourself as a smart person. Majority opinion is often wrong."

—Red Green

Men Always Need Something to Do

I have golfing buddies. They're good guys. We golf every Friday afternoon and we all get along just fine. But I think if you took those same four guys and put them into a car or sat them at a restaurant table or parked them on a bench for those same four hours, there would eventually be bickering and fleeting homicidal thoughts. This is because men have trouble socializing with each other when there's nothing else to do. Put them together at a ball game or a racetrack or a golf course and everything's fine. Women on the other hand seem the complete opposite. They've been known to turn a television off in favor of conversation. They often spend a couple of hours over a cup of coffee with a friend. They work from a different set of rules than we do. Conversation can never be the central focus for us. None of us has all that much to say and even less interest in hearing what the other guy has on his mind. That's why golf is such a great game for men. It's the perfect way to feign interest in your friends without wasting a whole afternoon.

Bed & Breakfast Blues

We have a couple of friends who have retired from their jobs and have turned their house into a bed and breakfast. So naturally, my wife and I end up discussing the possibility of doing the same thing. That's a natural reaction. Whenever someone you know does something that you haven't done, you start considering it. That's why when you're selling some product that's completely worthless, the first sale is so important. Now, I don't know if my wife is going to push this bed and breakfast thing, but I plan to fight it all the way. I don't like strangers in my house at any time, and staying overnight is really asking for trouble. I'm going to hear strange noises and snippets of conversations and only imagine what's going on in there. And who came up with the concept of giving them breakfast? That's not the high point of my day, either physically or emotionally. I'll be awake all night listening to potential tribal rituals and then I'm expected to greet these transients at the bottom of the stairs with a smile and an omelet. It's more than a coincidence that the emergence of bed and breakfasts is concurrent with the increase in domestic violence.

Hardware 10, Software 2

These days there is a great deal of emphasis placed on communication and interaction. We have cell phones and pagers and e-mail and networking. We have all of this technology allowing us to exchange ideas easily and instantly. So what are we doing with it? We're calling people when we don't need to. We're programming our cell phones to play tunes instead of ringing. We're getting non-essential messages in a variety of formats. We're playing internet computer games at our desks with strangers from around the world. We haven't really improved communication—we've just made it easier for bad ideas to be shared. Before the techno revolution, if you had a theory, you presented it to a friend or a colleague first to see if it had merit. You could limit the embarrassment. Now if you have a theory, you create a website and broadcast it to the world. Life gets very difficult when everybody knows you're an idiot. It's bad enough when it's just your wife.

Non Cogito Ergo Sum

Thinking is usually a good thing. It can save you from physical harm and psychological damage. But thinking at the wrong time can also create a lot of problems. Here is a short list of times when it's better not to think:

- When you're being rolled in for surgery.
- When you're being disciplined by a loved one.
- When you're watching an approaching hockey puck.
- When you're undergoing a tax audit.
- When you're at a wrestling match.
- When you're getting directions.
- When you're assembling an explosive device.
- When your spouse is telling you what to wear.
- When you're asked for an opinion.
- When you're at a board meeting.
- Whenever you're feeling smart.

We're Better When We're Losing

I don't know whether this is just a male thing but I find I do my best work and make my best efforts when I'm in trouble. When everything's going well and I'm cruising, I just let it all slide, but as soon as my boss is making threatening noises or my wife pulls out her suitcase or the police start nosing around, well, that's when I get it together. I'm also nicer when I'm behind the eight ball. When things are going well I get arrogant because to me that's what success is all about.

Why do we have such a strange behavioral pattern? I think when you boil it all down, it stems from the inner conflict of being congenitally lazy but not wanting to look like an idiot. That's why competition works. It's not about winning. It's about the fear of losing and letting the world in on your secret regarding your personal proficiency and work ethic. They say if you want to get something done, take it to someone who's busy. I say if you want to get something done, take it to someone who's in deep trouble.

Quote of the Day

"Don't let that cramp bother you. It means you must still have a muscle."

—*Red Green*

Life Lessons Part 1

As I look back over my life so far, I've learned a few life lessons. Some of them were expected. You could see them coming. Others came as a total surprise. So to enlighten those who are coming after me, here are a few unexpected life lessons that you may encounter:

- Jokes that are funny to you may not be funny to members of the opposite sex or the clergy.

- A t-shirt saying "I'm with stupid" should never be worn on a first date.

- Clearing your nasal passages should be done in private, rather than during a job interview.

- Women have no interest in how much you can drink.

- Teenagers with purple hair are not seeking your approval.

- Spring-loaded tools should never be carried in the pants pockets.

Now Is the End, Perish the World

I heard on the news that there's a day coming over the next few months when several of the planets are going to align themselves with Mars (which I think was a hit for the Fifth Dimension) and it occurred to me that some cult group is going to predict that day will be the end of the world. And that we should all prepare. I'm not exactly sure what that means. I wouldn't know what to pack for a world termination. I guess something loose-fitting and sensible shoes. Okay, that's a little glib, but I don't honestly think the world-ending thing is going to happen. So instead of the rest of us preparing for the world to end, I suggest these fanatics should maybe prepare for the world not to end. What then? What if we hit the stroke of midnight and there's no horrific conflagration? Don't you think they should prepare for that? Maybe it's time to engage in a new activity—might I humbly suggest rational thought.

Silence Please

In my early twenties, I was in a rock band. We played different kinds of music but all of it really loud. The slogan "How do we do it? Volume!" was a pretty good description of our approach. When you're loud, you don't get criticized. Or at least you don't hear it. But that was thirty years ago. Now I don't like anything loud. I need to be able to hear what my wife is saying. I've learned that it's better for everyone if I hear her the first time. Before I buy something else that we don't need. And before she commits me to a social function. Or an institution. I used to like loud things like rock music and dragsters and explosions. Now I like quiet things—like babies not crying and phones not ringing and salesmen not knocking. If I worked at the airport wearing those silencer earmuffs, I'd probably leave them on all the time. Except of course when my wife is talking.

We Need a Possession Chain

The Food Chain has been in existence for millions of years and works well. I think we should apply the same approach to our levels of conspicuous consumption. We need a Possession Chain: a table that shows us the order of acquiring products and services. For example, you start with a toaster and then in time you move up to a toaster oven and then eventually a microwave. Starting with a microwave is in conflict with the Laws of Nature and will lead to unhappiness and badly burnt popcorn. Likewise, if you live in a $25,000 home, you shouldn't be driving a $30,000 car. It will only make you unhappy or it will make the person you live with unhappy, which will eventually affect you through the Trickle-Down Theory. Here's a rough guide to show you the order in which men should spend their money: home, car, boat, motorcycle, snow machine, riding mower, Seadoo, bush buggy, hovercraft, backhoe, helicopter, new suit, divorce lawyer.

Survival of the Fittest

I like to watch boxing on television. I like the raw confrontation of it but if either of the combatants gets cut or hurt, I immediately feel awful and change the channel. I'd never want to watch a fight live. And when people ask me what I like about boxing, I have to admit it's the best example of one of Nature's basic laws—Survival of the Fittest. But now I'm thinking that law needs to be changed. Survival of the fittest is fine for a one-on-one battle, but when it's part of a round robin tournament that could conceivably be expanded to include everyone in the world, you'd end up with one sole survivor. One earth person who, although being of supreme physical and mental capability, would not be able to procreate. Since Survival of the Fittest in its ultimate form is politically incorrect and leads to the end of the Human Race, I suggest we change it to Temporary Setback of the Less Fit—who are probably nicer people for it.

Dumbing Down in Self-Defense

The expression "dumbing down" is one I hear a lot these days. And people are worried about it. They consider dumbing down to be a form of pandering to the lowest common denominator and the inference is that people are so stupid these days that you have to lower your intelligence level to speak to them. I don't agree. I think the average person is smarter than ever before in history. You have to be. You have to be able to communicate with computers. The manuals are three inches thick—there's a clue. Nobody from the Middle Ages or even the Industrial Revolution could have handled that. They couldn't even remember their PIN numbers. We've got voice mail, e-mail, faxes, wireless, two-way, electronic ticketing, and on and on. Do you think Leonardo da Vinci could program a VCR? No. We're not dumb. We're smart.

But we're tired of being smart. We need a break. We need to be dumb once in a while so our brains don't cramp. And if these big companies weren't run by nerds, they'd understand that. Thinking is necessary—but it's not fun. That's why smart people are boring at parties. So get with the program. Think for show but dumb down for dough.

You've Done a Lot By Comparison

It's human nature to compare ourselves with others, but sometimes, as we get older, in order to feel we haven't done badly, we need to look outside our own race or even species. For example, the Giant Sea Turtle lives 150 years and its only accomplishment of any significance comes from laying eggs in the sand. You do that every month in the boardroom and you probably won't make it past 75. Or look at those giant redwood sequoia trees or whatever they're called. They're about 1,200 years old and they're famous because people drive through them. Well you let people walk all over you and you're only 47. So I say you're doing just fine. Maybe if you lived to be 250 we could expect more, but let's not wish for too much of a good thing.

Quote of the Day

"I'm not paranoid because it scares me to even think about it."

—Red Green

Let's Be Sensitive About Sensitivity

Men have been under a lot of pressure for the last thirty years or so to get more in touch with their feelings. To be more sensitive and to let their feminine side come out. I guess it's a good thing, I don't know. My wife's all for it so that's pretty much the clincher around our house.

But there have been some downsides. That whole strong silent macho thing has been replaced by a bunch of gushy guys who dance just a little too well for my liking. And men who ordinarily never say anything have gotten in touch with their feelings, only to realize that their feelings are hurt. So they start whining. About everything. It's amazing how hundreds of years of repressed self-expression can backlash into tirades on everything from the weather to squeegee kids. Let's be careful how we use our newfound outgoing sensitivity. Some of the best male actors ever were a lot better in the silent movies than they were in the talkies.

Signs That You Need a Vacation

A lot of people are working too hard these days. Here are some danger signs to watch for:

- You always look like you've had seven coffees.

- You come home from work and your entire family has their bathing suits on.

- You only ride elevators that feature reggae music.

- You put a tiny umbrella into your glass of Maalox.

- You look for a tie that goes with your Hawaiian shirt.

- You have money in the bank.

- You make Johnny Winter look tanned.

- When you smile your wife doesn't recognize you.

Kind Of Interesting

Over the years, the phrase "kind of" has made its way into our vernacular. While the meaning of the phrase is not completely clear, I think you have to use it with caution. Here is a list of questions to which the answer "kind of" is inappropriate:

- Do you love me?

- Do you swear to tell the truth and nothing but the truth?

- Are you pregnant?

- Do you have a job?

- Does this car belong to you?

- Did you pay your Income Tax?

- Are you a doctor?

- Have you been faithful?

- Are you the father of this child?

Man She Looks Good

I was in a golf tournament recently and I couldn't help noticing that the young lady in the refreshment cart was significantly under-dressed. I'm not complaining. I'm just saying I didn't know where to look. Well actually I did know where to look, I just didn't think I could get away with it.

I understand that people dress that way to attract the attention of the opposite sex, especially in their own age group. But this was a golf tournament made up of mostly old guys like myself so I figure her outfit was mainly a marketing ploy. And it was working. She was doing a brisk business and her tip jar was just one more thing about her that was full to overflowing.

There were no victims here, so I decided to feel good about it. I'm going to treat it as a medical check-up. If I can look at a beautiful young woman and have an emotional response, that means my body is still working. And if I can do that without in any way thinking she might find me attractive, that means my brain must be okay too.

Me Tarzan, You Technology

Technology has allowed me to pick up some new bad habits. One of them is "voice mail." If I'm too busy to answer the phone, I don't. I just let it kick over to voice mail with the idea that I'll call them back later. Sometimes I even check the "Caller I.D." to make sure it's nobody important. Once in a while I check the messages and then re-save them because I'm too busy to call back right then but I'll do it soon. It's like the VCR. I don't have time to watch the shows I like, so I tape them only to find out I don't have time to watch them later either.

Now of course the fundamental problem here is that technology hasn't addressed the real problem, which is: how do you slow down time? We don't need voice mail and VCRs that allow us to postpone commitments. We need a way to stretch time so we can do everything we want. Otherwise, I'm going to have to cut down on the number of television shows I like and also on the number of friends and associates who call me and leave messages. I'm starting to get the feeling that technology's ultimate goal is to prevent us from having friends and fun.

You're Not Fooling Anyone

You may pretend to be young and in the know, but be careful. There are several things that can give you away:

- You buy a drink for a young lady at the end of the bar and then fall asleep before it arrives.

- You're at your young girlfriend's apartment when the doorbell rings, and it takes you a full five minutes to get up out of the beanbag chair.

- Under your Tommy Hilfiger sweater is a Monkees Tour t-shirt.

- You quote one-liners from the Tonight Show when Jack Paar was the host.

- When politics is being discussed, you relate everything to Watergate.

- You have jet-black hair on your head and chin but there's a shocking tuft of gray coming out of your left nostril.

License to Thrill

We all have to face the day when we get so old we flunk our driver's test and are no longer allowed to drive a car. This can be a major blow to the ego, so I say start preparing to beat the system now. Buy a house in a golf community on waterfront property. Then get yourself a powerboat and a golf cart. Things that don't require licenses. And on your ninetieth birthday drop a racing engine into the golf cart. Then cruise the neighborhood trying to pick up women. Preferably golfers.

Take a Pause For the Cause

As I get older, I find that I'm not as quick to respond as I used to be. And I don't just mean in the bedroom. I mean conversationally. I remember the days when if somebody asked a question or made a controversial statement, I'd jump in there with both feet to express my opinion. I don't do that anymore. My enthusiasm for saying what I think has been dampened by experience. A married man or anyone else in middle management will tell you that there is great value in silence. The person who's talking to you will assume you're thinking very carefully about your response. They'll find that flattering. They don't need to know that you're actually trying to conceal your response and are taking extra time hoping they'll forget the question. If you ever have to testify in court, your lawyer will tell you to take your time and think over your answer carefully before you speak. That's good advice for daily living because you are on trial constantly. And as soon as you testify, you have to be prepared for cross-examination.

So Many Cars, So Few Lanes

It's always good when you can take something unpleasant and find some value in it. Like being at a family reunion and finding that cousin who owes you money. So I was thinking that if you commute to the big smoke everyday and you're stuck in traffic for hours at a time, this is an excellent opportunity to shop for a car. You see which ones have the best acceleration. And brakes. And then acceleration again. You see which ones handle the best when switching lanes quickly or going into a four-wheel drift on the gravel shoulder. If you see a car pulled over in a radar trap, that means it has a good engine but poor visibility. You also get a chance to do a market survey. For example, if you see a preponderance of Hondas, that means they probably have good resale value based on their popularity, and you'll always be able to find parts, even at the side of the road. So, instead of cursing rush hour, use it to do research for your next automotive purchase. (This technique works best when done from the window of a commuter train.)

The Dark Side of Competence

Often in life, what we're told flies in the face of what we know to be true. For example, in the area of professionalism and competency, we are told that everyone wants you to excel in these areas and that whatever you do in life, it is your duty to do it to the best of your ability. I don't think that's entirely true. Oh sure, when you need something like open-heart surgery you want the surgeon to be competent and professional. But when the activity doesn't affect you in any way, like watching your neighbor having a pool installed, you enjoy it more if the bobcat operator is incompetent and amateurish. That's because competence is boring. Whereas incompetence is always interesting. And when it doesn't negatively impact your life, it's downright entertaining. So, if you're hiring someone to fill a useless redundant position in your company, go with the bumbling incompetent. They'll give everybody a lot of laughs and they'll never quit to go to a better job.

It's Time to Move On

There are times in life when it's better not to stop, but to keep moving. In fact, you might even want to pick up the pace. Situations like these:

- There's a hint of methane in the air and it's your turn to hold the baby.

- Mike Wallace is waiting to see you in your office.

- As you arrive at your neighbor's house party, you see a large display of cleaning products.

- Young people in suits with books under their arms are standing on your front porch.

- A heavyset man on the beach is taking off his robe.

- You see a hitchhiker dressed as Captain Kirk.

- You see a hitchhiker dressed as William Shatner.

- You see William Shatner.

Stuff Happens

I am by nature an optimist (or at least I hope I am) but there is something very empowering about removing unrealistic expectation from your life. Maybe when I was a young person I could bite off more than I could chew because I could hold it in my cheek for twenty years to soften it up. I don't have that kind of time anymore, so now I try to make my projections with a stronger bulb. I've stopped expecting people to do what I want. Bad weather doesn't surprise me. And I no longer make major purchases based solely on my ability to come up with the down payment.

Quote of the Day

"Age doesn't always bring wisdom. Sometimes age comes alone."

—*Red Green*

Trafficking

I was driving in the middle of a pack of cars on the highway this week. We were all speeding. No problem. Suddenly a police car pulled on to the highway and we all hit the brakes, trying to subtly ease our way down to the speed limit. Luckily, the cop didn't notice. He just thought his car must have tremendous power to be able to catch up to all of us that quickly. So we all moved at the same speed in a huge mass joined together by guilt. Thankfully the cop got off a couple of exits later and we could all get back to breaking the law. We're not criminals. We just think that there are a couple of laws that you only obey when a policeman is present. So when they're around we pretend we always drive at a safe speed. And they pretend to believe us. It's kind of an unspoken agreement between the two sides—like not swearing in front of your kids and vice versa.

Time Changes Everything

Einstein proved that time is relative. It's a theory that becomes more relevant as we age. I'd try anything in my twenties because I knew I had lots of time to heal or apologize or do community service. But now I'm very fussy about what I spend my time doing. I'm running out of it so it's becoming much more valuable. I used to view life as a timeless adventure. "What do you want to do?" "I don't know, what do you want to do?" Now I treat it as a conjugal visit. "Let's get this over with, I need my sleep."

Quote of the Day

"Forget the health food. I need all the preservatives I can get."

—*Red Green*

Signs That It's Time for You to Stop Talking

Whenever you're talking to someone it's important to watch their body language to make sure they consider the conversation a worthwhile investment of their time because you may want to speak with them again in the future. Here are a few signs to watch for. Signs that may indicate it's time for you to stop talking.

- The other person makes that "yak yak yak" hand gesture while you're talking.

- They turn their back to you and stare at the wall.

- They blink and their eyes stay shut.

- They grab their nose and look at you accusingly.

- They pretend to see someone they know in the distance even though you're shipwrecked on a desert island.

- They excuse themselves to take a call on their cell phone, which is actually an ashtray.

- They swallow a pickled egg whole so they can be rushed to the hospital.

- They reach to their side hoping to find a holstered gun.

Taking the BS Out of CEO

As I was washing a thin layer of ash and metal particulate off my boat last week, I got thinking about pollution and how people will say anything for money. Yes, the CEO of that big factory insists that all of their emissions are inert and harmless. But he says that from his hermetically sealed office just before jumping into his $200,000 Mercedes and speeding home to his million-dollar house which is forty miles away and upwind. Well I've come up with a plan to make sure these people are telling us the truth. The Queen has to live in Buckingham Palace, The President has to live in the White House, ministers have to live in the manse. It comes with the job. I say that CEOs of polluting companies should have to live on the grounds of their own factories. That would cut through the rhetoric pretty fast. Ordering people to live in the hub of the environment they create is a great way to force them to be honest. (With the apparent exception of the White House.)

The Value of New Old Friends

I made a new friend recently who's six years older than me. He's bright and fit and has all of his hair. He may even have some of mine. He's witty and laughs easily and the women seem to warm to him. Other guys in my situation might be jealous, but not me. This guy gives me hope. I think to myself that when I get to be his age, I'll be just like that. I get thinking that the current balding, overweight, boring me is just a phase I'm going through and if I can just wait it out by finding an interesting hobby like watching television, then I'll eventually change from being a slug in a grungy cocoon to being a stylish butterfly like my new buddy. Maybe old age is like going through puberty. But in reverse.

Quote of the Day

"When your son finally leaves home, you'll find there's now plenty of hot water but you're the one who's in it."

—Red Green

Gifts With a Message

Most of us get gifts on our birthday or at Christmas, and, over time, it can be an expected thing that we just take for granted. Don't do it. Always take a close look at any gift because it often signals a message that you might otherwise miss. Here is a list of gifts that have hidden messages:

- A full-length mirror.
- A comb.
- Dry-cleaning coupons.
- A car air freshener.
- A tube of whitening toothpaste.
- A dog training video.
- A job offer in Africa.
- A skateboard.
- Nose hair clippers.
- A gift pack of bath soap and disinfectant.
- A lawnmower.

Keeping It in the Family

Nothing is all good or all bad. It's always a mix of the two in various quantities. Even good manners can have a bad side. I'm thinking about the good manners of not arguing with a family member who is always spouting off his theories of human behavior and galactic interaction. I know it may be impolite to disagree, but, by saying nothing, we are implying to Uncle Bob that we agree with him, and that can be a very dangerous message. His ridiculous viewpoints get even more entrenched and his determination to express them increases. When you see a loudmouth in person or on television, you can be pretty sure he comes from a family who was just too darned polite for their own good. So, if you've got someone like that in your house, please be rude to them at every opportunity. Otherwise you're forcing the rest of us to do it for you, and that's not polite.

Quote of the Day

"The quickest way to get the contempt of strangers is to drive at the speed limit."

—*Red Green*

Testosterone-Phobia

I know that there are many factors that make a person what they are, but chemistry has to be a big part of it. And if you're a man, testosterone must be the most influential chemical. You take a normal man and drastically reduce his testosterone level and you either get an ugly woman or a guy who walks funny and never shaves. Testosterone is a key ingredient in the man recipe, and that's why I'm concerned about the negative messages that we see every day, targeting testosterone. For example, animals being neutered. Now I can understand the rationale of castrating pigs to fatten them up on the basis that they'll eat more if they have nothing else to think about, but the idea of having your dog neutered to make him more manageable upsets me. Some days I'm a little unmanageable myself, and I don't want my wife looking at our friendly obedient dog and getting ideas.

No Need to Explain Even If You Could

There are many great things about being married to the same person for a long time and I'm a grateful husband on a fairly regular basis. One of the best perks is the evolution of the communication level between two people over time. It reaches the point where words are unnecessary. What a bonus. Life is hard enough, but having to explain every little setback or accident or why the police are in the driveway can get very tedious. I truly appreciate being able to just go quietly to bed with a couple of aspirins and a cold compress. It's great to be with someone who knows you so well, you don't need to come up with an explanation. The down side of that relationship is that when you've screwed up so bad that you do have to come up with an explanation, it better be a dandy.

For Men Only

While men and women are doing more things together than ever, which is a good thing, there is obviously still a need for each sex to spend time with their own kind—to be with people who share your physiology and experiences and, in many cases, your attitudes. Women seem to do this much better than we do. They have shopping trips or quilting bees or sleepovers. The list for men is less impressive—hunting and fishing. Like we have to be killing something to have a good time. And men having a sleepover really gets the rumor mill going. So, instead, why don't we start a club for men only where we could relax and be ourselves and bond? Here are some suggested features:

- **The TV Room**—built on top of an open Dumpster. The television screen occupies one whole wall and everybody gets a remote.

- **The BS Lounge**—you're allowed to tell any story you want and nobody has to pretend to believe it.

- **The Observation Room**—men sit in elevated bleachers and watch other members assemble items without reading the instructions.

- **The Garage**—men lean under the open hood of a car, beer in hand, staring blankly at the fuel injection system.

- **The Model Room**—a pool for racing model boats and a slot car track. Reckless speed with limited liability.

- **The Decompression Room**—no eye contact. No talking. No chairs facing each other.

- **The Hot Stove Lounge**—a place to burn things—trees, old furniture, unsuccessful projects.

- **The Underwear Room**—relaxed dress code.

To See Ourselves As Others See Us

I was at a social event and a middle-aged fat bald guy was pointing out all of the beautiful young single women who were at the event. And he capped it off with, "Just my luck, I'm married." And he was so right.

Quote of the Day

"One of the upsides of getting older is that you are never suspected of any crime that required agility, strength, speed or cunning."

—Red Green

Beware of the Shopper

If you live with someone who's an avid shopper, you may need to be extra careful with your appearance and behavior. A person who shops a lot knows the importance of comparing features and options and is completely focused on getting good value. And the scariest part is that they continue to comparison shop even after they've bought the item. If they see something they like better or if the product doesn't perform as advertised, they have no qualms about taking it back for a refund. This can be a dangerous pattern if you happen to be the husband of such a person. My advice is for you to see yourself as a used car. You can go one of two ways. You can either try to convince your wife that you have retained so much of your original value that she'd never find a better unit of your vintage. Or you can convince her that you have zero trade-in value and the only way she'll get her money out of you is to run you into the ground.

Civilization Begins at Home

I heard on the radio this week that scientists are looking for house designs that would work well on Mars. The inference is that we're going to live on Mars soon because Earth is getting overpopulated. I beg to differ. New York and Toronto may be overpopulated, but have you been to Alaska lately? We have lots of room left right here on Earth. It's just that most of our available space doesn't have perfect weather or soil and isn't close to a major highway or an indoor mall. But then, neither is Mars, and it's a heck of a commute. Maybe one day some of us will live there, but I'd take a hard look at Baffin Island first.

Work with What You Have

You can't do a lot about your basic physical appearance, but you can enhance how you look by the way you dress and the environment in which you place yourself. Here are a few examples:

- If you're short, fill your garden with dwarf plants and stand by the ceramic leprechaun.

- If you're on the heavy side, hang out near short wide buildings.

- If you're extra tall, look up all the time.

- If your eyes are crossed, paint something interesting on the end of your nose.

- If you're very thin, lean on telephone poles.

- If your teeth are yellow, dye your beard brown.

- If you have halitosis, exhale slowly upwind.

- The uglier you are, the more cologne you should wear.

- The more wrinkled you are, the more ironed your clothes have to be.

A Love to Dye For

I know a lot of guys my age are dyeing their hair. That's fine. I think it's important for people to look their best, but there is a risk involved. If you succeed in making yourself look younger, it will attract younger people to you. Younger friends and co-workers and even potential love interests will gravitate towards you, and that could create problems. These friends and co-workers will want to do things that are completely outside your experience. You'll be in trouble. You can't fake skydiving. And it's even worse with a love interest. You can't fake anything. And the last thing you need is a young girlfriend that will cut into your hair-dyeing time. With luck, she'll actually turn out to be a woman your own age who also dyes her hair. That will give you both a common interest and something you can do together on the weekends.

Protesting Too Much

I was doing something on my computer the other day when suddenly a notice pops up in the middle of the screen saying, "You have performed an illegal operation! This program will be shut down!" What is that? An illegal operation? I pressed a button on my computer. Is that against the law now? This seems way over the top to me. I think it's a device created by the people who make these computers to cover their own mistakes. Obviously there's a glitch in the software which triggers a problem, but instead of creating a sign that says, "We screwed up by selling you this computer before we got the bugs out of it," they went with "You have performed an illegal operation!" It's not a bad move actually. Maybe you should try that in your life. When your wife criticizes you, you just say, "You have performed an illegal operation! This conversation will be shut down!" And then go out. But first, make sure you have a house key in your pocket.

Quote of the Day

"A bird in the hand is only better than two in the bush if you like birds. I've always preferred two in the bush."

—*Red Green*

Pay Now, Pay Later

I've been a consumer for a pretty long time and, except for a brief hiatus in the early nineties, I've done my part. I've bought my share of cars and boats and homes and appliances and tools. I've had situations where I felt I paid too much and at other times I thought I got a real deal but, over time, I've come to the conclusion that everything costs the same. For example, you can either pay top dollar for a high-quality used car and have years

of trouble-free driving, or you can buy some cheap beater and spend a fortune on repairs and tow trucks. Same with boats. Same with everything. My advice is to decide on the exact make and model you want and then shop for the best price on that, rather than buying the cheapest make and model you can find, and then having to talk yourself into liking it. I'm very fond of this theory and truly wish I could afford it.

Fatal Attractiveness

As we get older, it gets more and more difficult to attract women. We lose our physique and our hair. We wear glasses and hearing aids and we forget what we were saying in mid-sentence. It eventually gets so bad, your only hope to attract a member of the opposite sex is to make sure you smell good and then sit near a woman with a big nose.

Quote of the Day

"If you find yourself feeling happy, try not to think of anything."

—Red Green

Things That Go Fast

Everything seems to be going faster and faster. Cars and rockets and people's lives. I think Einstein proved that everything is relative or something like that and it's never truer than it is with speed. Now that I've lived a bit, I have a better perspective on what rate of motion is. Here's a list of things that really do go fast:

- Knees.
- Cash.
- Spicy food.
- Time spent in the proctologist's waiting room.
- The time between your birthdays.
- Your engagement.
- Your honeymoon.
- Your new car warranty.
- Your moments of brilliance.
- Your hairline.
- Your waistline
- Your timeline.

Early Parole for Low Handicap Golfers Only

There's a lot of discussion about early parole for serious offenders and the big question is whether or not they are fully rehabilitated. I have a suggestion. Allow these prisoners to play golf for at least six months prior to their parole application. If they can get their handicap down under 15, then they should be set free. If not, they have no control over their bodies and parole should be denied. If this rule were ever applied to me, I would spend my entire life behind bars—which, in some ways, would be kinder than allowing me to play golf.

Quote of the Day

"Employees who never ask for a raise are probably stealing from you."

—*Red Green*

We're Getting Too Comfortable

Every generation gets a little wimpier than the one before it. Our ancestors lived in wooden shacks without running water or electricity. We have central heat, central air, central vac, central casting, humidifiers, dehumidifiers, carbon filters, ozone detectors, smoke detectors, chest protectors, bomb deflectors, and house inspectors. We can push one button in our house and another in our car and as long as we have an attached garage, we will never leave an atmosphere of constant temperature, humidity, oxygen content, and clarity. It makes for an easy, comfortable life, but, over time, Mother Nature will devolve us to the point where we can't handle any change in our environment. Sure it might be nice to never shiver or sweat—but not if it means that every time you open the fridge or oven door, you have a massive cardiac infarction. So don't try so hard to make it so easy. Human beings survive a lot better when they have something to fight against. That's why married people live longer.

Techno-Babylon

There is a misconception out there that says technology makes us more efficient. That it saves us time. I don't agree. Yes, a microwave oven can reheat a slice of pizza faster and more efficiently than a normal oven, but first I have to go out and earn enough money to buy the microwave, so you have to add that time in. Then I have to read the instructions and set the clock. Then I have to pay for the electricity to run it. I know you're going to say "not as much electricity as a stove uses." Don't worry about it. I'll eat the pizza cold. That's faster than any microwave and it doesn't cost a cent. So be careful when you're choosing technology. If it's something you really need in your life, great. But a lot of technology just gives us faster ways of doing unnecessary jobs.

Five Questions That Scare Married Men

- Did you do what you promised to do?
- Where did the apple pie go?
- Do you remember what today is?
- What size pants are you wearing these days?
- Have you got big plans for later?

Dressing for Trouble

I sometimes take abuse for my wardrobe. I tend to be on the low side of casual. Tattered jeans and a flannel shirt is my uniform of choice. It's not an unconscious choice. I'm very aware of why I dress like that. First of all, I think it sends out a good message: that I'm not using my clothes to make you think I'm rich or important. I'm important to me, and while I'm happy to have you join me in that, it's your call. It also sends a message to single women that I'm out of bounds. If I dress this shabby while I'm looking, can you imagine how bad it will get once you get to know me? (My wife has never totally bought this argument.) But the main reason I dress this way is because I think you have to be ready for anything: a leaky pipe, a lawnmower that won't start, or a car that needs a push. When there's an emergency I can just jump right in. I don't need to find a phone booth to change in. So when you see a guy decked out in extra-casual-wear, he's dressed for battle. And when you see a guy in an expensive suit, he may have money, but if you have an emergency, he'll be grabbing his cell phone and calling somebody like me.

Coming Out of the Closet

I'm having a problem with my closet these days. It's full of clothes that I never wear. I spent an hour or so looking at the situation, trying to figure out what went wrong, and it seems to be a combination of factors. First of all, there are the clothes that my wife has bought for me. These tend to be at the stylish, suave, Euro-dork end of the spectrum and are always bought when she's been to a movie or read a romance novel and has forgotten what I look like. Then there are the clothes that I bought while shopping with my wife. These purchases are always made in a hurry, without trying anything on, and for the sole purpose of satisfying her and getting out of the store as quickly as possible. Then we have a small group of clothes that actually fit me but that I refuse to wear because they're made for a much fatter, older man. That leaves us with the clothes that I actually do wear and they're all at least ten years old. They tend to be a little tight and I have to suck my stomach in so hard that I sometimes get back spasms. But I hate to throw them out because guys like me prefer a wardrobe that's been lived in. So instead, I have a plan. All I need to do is meet a guy my age who's my height but ten pounds heavier than me. I'll throw out everything I have now and buy all of his old clothes.

Credit Where Credit Is Due

They have sophisticated computers in cars these days. Things like the GPS that tells you exactly how to get to where you're going, for anyone who doesn't have a wife. Or the central monitoring unit that tells you if there's a door open or a seatbelt undone or your engine just fell out. I'm thinking they could easily devise a computer that kept track of how fast you're going compared to the speed limit. For example, if you're driving to work and the speed limit is 60, but you're only going 30 because the traffic is so bad, that would be registered in the computer. Let's say you did that for fifteen minutes. The computer would show that as a credit on the dashboard screen. That means that as soon as you hit an open stretch of road, you'd be allowed to use that credit without getting a speeding ticket. You could go 90 for 15 minutes or 120 for 7½ minutes or 150 for 3¾ minutes or the speed of light for a nanosecond. As soon as your credit was used up, you would resume the speed limit. I know this would never work but it's nice to dream about.

When Not to Say What You're Thinking

- While the policeman is writing out the ticket.

- When your Minister asks if you know any good jokes.

- While you're at your in-laws' house sitting at the dining room table staring at the contents of your dinner plate.

- When the boss asks how you like his haircut.

- When your wife says, "What's your problem?"

Forgive and Forget

I've always had difficulty with the phrase "Forgive and forget." I think it's a great ideal but it's one those phrases like "I promise I'll respect you in the morning." It seldom happens. I'm just not spiritually evolved enough to forgive and forget. I was feeling bad about that until I realized that it's not really necessary to forgive and forget. All you have to do is forget. If you can forget that somebody did something, that's good enough. You don't have to forgive them. You have no idea what you'd even be forgiving them for. This has given me new hope. Forgiving has always been difficult, but forgetting is something I just seem to get better and better at.

Quote of the Day

"If you smile at everyone you meet, they will eventually suspect you of something"

—*Red Green*

Nice Trophy Case

You see these old guys with the young ex-model wives. You know the ones I mean. He's a shriveled up billionaire and she's gorgeous and the same age as his socks. They call them "trophy wives." A little something to have on your arm to let the other guys know that you have more to offer at 90 than they do at 27. (You may have more to offer—but not for nearly as long.)

So okay, I can understand the trophy concept from the old guy's point of view; I just don't see the appeal for the woman. Now if it's love, that's fine. Logic and love rarely intersect. But if it's something else, then it seems to me that this old codger is a "trophy husband" for her. Some trophy. I've got bowling awards that look better than most of these guys. I'm thinking that these woman are more attracted to the safety and security of a rich grandfather-type than they are to the good looks and virility of a man their own age. And I guess when he passes on in a year or two, she just finds another one like him. There are a lot of rich old guys who find young women attractive. But it takes some-one special to be a career "trophy wife." You need the personal-ity of a nurse and a bunch of black dresses.

Cars of the Future

I'm looking to buy a new car in the near future and it's turning into a real life moment for me. I've started to realize that since they're making cars that last ten years, I won't need a whole lot more of them. That changes everything. That means that I'd better make sure I get a car that I feel good about. I don't want to end my days in a Yugo. No, I'm thinking I'd better get that sports car I've always wanted. The clock is ticking here. So I went looking at Corvettes and Vipers, that kind of thing. I noticed the salesman trying to look away as I struggled for a full five minutes to get into the vehicle. But that was like an eyeblink compared to the time it took me to get out. And while I was in there, about three inches off the ground in the prone position, I didn't look like a macho racer at the Indy 500. I looked like an old guy on a stretcher. People would think I was driving my grandson's car. And on the self-preservation level, bad things happen when reflexes like mine are going 150 miles an hour. I'm calling the salesman today and ordering a small gutless sedan with plastic doors and airbags. Please don't say, "You are what you drive."

Keeping the Magic Alive

If you're a married man and you're hoping to stay that way, I think it's a good idea to do everything you can to maintain your value in your wife's eyes. You should treat yourself the same way you would look after a car you plan to keep for a long time. Wash and wax as often as you can. Change the oil once a month. No quick starts or stops and keep the mileage down. That'll take care of your physical appearance—but to get to the heart and mind of a woman, you need to have a little mystique working for you. Instead of having an affair, just pretend you are. Have women call you at home and then hang up when your wife answers. Throw a tube of passion-pink lipstick into your glove compartment. Speak French in your sleep. Life is an auction and nothing increases the value of an item more than the fear that someone else is bidding. And when your wife finds out that you're actually not cheating on her she'll have a huge victory celebration and you'll be the guest of honor. Rest up.

Point and Click

I've noticed that, when I ask my computer to do something by pointing at an icon and clicking on it, it will try for thirty seconds or so, and then tell me it failed and just go back to where it was. No guilt. No attitude. It doesn't kick anything or hurt itself. I envy that. I'm not like a computer at all. You can't just point and click to make me try something. In fact, the more you point, the less I click. And once I do try something, I don't quit. I just keep working at it until I keel over or the thing I'm working on explodes in a fireball. That's because once I start something, I'd rather get incredibly angry than stop. I have attitude. I kick things. I hurt myself. If my computer could see me it would say, "You have performed an illegal operation." Maybe one day I'll turn into a computer and everything will be okay. But for that to happen, I'll need a lot more memory.

Teach by Bad Example

We have all these biographies in print and on television that highlight the lives of very successful famous people. Over time, this constant exposure to people who have excelled makes us feel like total losers. I say we start featuring the stories of abject failures. The Esperanto teacher or the Yugo salesman or that guy up the street with the emu. It's time to feel good about ourselves again.

Quote of the Day

"Body parts are like members of a large family. They start out as a team, but as they get older, they each do whatever the heck they want."

—*Red Green*

Be a Handyman

I have this theory that the human brain is a muscle rather than an organ. And as a muscle, it gets stronger with use and, conversely, atrophies through idleness. People who don't do any thinking in their lives as a way of keeping their brain fresh for old age are seriously misinformed. You're much better off to use your brain as often as possible. Even once or twice a day if you can manage it.

And of course, choosing what to use your brain on is very important. You don't want to waste your time on things that are irrelevant or boring or beyond your comprehension. For most of us, things like abstract mathematics and nuclear physics are a complete waste of time.

I recommend that you become a Handyman. The mental agility required to diagnose why the refrigerator isn't working and then to acquire the correct part, remove the old one without breaking everything around it, and then install the new one, is a fantastic exercise. Not to mention what pinching your thumb in the door hinge does for your language skills. Then there's the whole creative challenge of explaining to your wife why the refrigerator couldn't be fixed, and thank goodness you didn't waste money by bringing in a professional repairman. These are the kind of skills that will keep your mind agile well into your old age. Plus you'll have a lot more free time, because your wife will refrain from telling you when something needs fixing.

New Lease on Life

I've just leased a car and I found the leasing options to be interesting. The payments are about the same as a car loan, but at the end of the term, I have more choices with the lease. With the loan, you may end up owning a car that you don't like. With a lease, that doesn't happen. So naturally I was wondering if you could expand the lease theory to include personal relationships. What if, instead of marrying a person, you just signed a three-year lease, and at the end of the term you could re-sign for another three years or unload the person privately or just walk away—as long as you hadn't had any accidents.

Quote of the Day

"This is one of those days I feel lucky to be alive... and so are the people I was barbecuing for."

—Red Green

Surveillance You Can Use

Now that we have satellites and miniature cameras and the crime rate seems to be under control, I'd like to see the whole surveillance industry become more service-oriented. Here are a few spy applications that I'd like to see:

- Let me see how unhappy all the girls who dumped me in high school are now.

- Let me hear what people say about me immediately after I leave the room.

- Let me see a room in my company where nobody ever goes, and is it big enough for a cot?

- Let me see my boss talking about me with his wife.

- Let me see my boss talking about anything with somebody else's wife.

- Let me see what's waiting for me when I come home late.

- Let me see what's waiting for me when I come home early.

Five Ways to Get Even

- When you know your teenage son is going to use your car, empty the gas tank and fill the back seat with fast food packages.

- When you're into your second hour of sitting in the doctor's office, sing "Tired of Waiting" by the Kinks at the top of your lungs.

- When your boss criticizes you in front of your fellow workers, yell back that you know what he's up to, but you don't find him even remotely attractive.

- Buy three sets of golf clubs and keep them together so they can see that you don't need to keep using ones that misbehave.

- While the cop is writing out your ticket, do an unflattering sketch of him and hand it to him when he's done.

The Bell Curve and You

I'm not exactly sure where I first found out about the Bell Curve. It was either high school Physics or Math. It had to do with averaging exam results so that a small number of people at the bottom failed, a small number of people at the top got really high marks and the bulk of us fell in between, in the big bulge part of the Bell Curve. In the naiveté of my youth, I thought that was pretty much it for the application of the Bell Curve. I've aged a lot since then. I've been able to apply the Bell Curve to almost every aspect of my life. In my job I've learned not to be so bad I'm at the bottom and get fired, or to be so good I'm at the top and get blamed. In my personal appearance, I've learned to strive for a mid-point between John Forsythe and Bobcat Goldthwaite. The same with my weight, fitness level and general behavioral patterns. Never good enough for the Nobel Prize. Never bad enough for long-term incarceration. I believe that true happiness lies at the center of the Bell Curve. If you look around your social circle and decide that you're at the bottom end of the Bell Curve, then you'd better start bringing people into the group who are actually worse than you, to improve your own position. That's what they do in most of the major corporations and political parties.

Pandora's Toolbox

Once in a while you have to call a repairman to come and fix something in your home. In most cases you don't know the guy and probably just picked his number out of the phone book. The problem, of course, is that you may be dealing with an incompetent who will create more problems than he corrects. Now, you don't want to be rude and ask him outright if he has any idea what he's doing, so here's a way to make a very quick judgment on the quality of the impending work. Hang around and look at the contents of his toolbox. If it contains any of the following, you may have a problem:

- Lots of bandages and painkillers.

- A handgun.

- F. Lee Bailey's business card.

- Only three tools, all hammers.

- A one-way plane ticket to Panama.

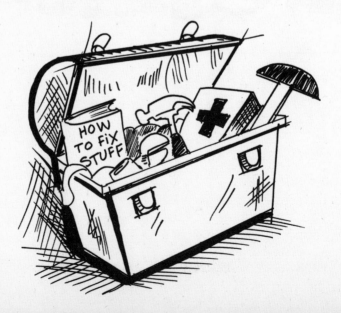

The Balance of Nature

I'm a great believer in maintaining a balance in the types of friends you cultivate. If you're a middle-aged married guy, it's important to hang out with an old married guy and a young engaged guy. That way you're ready to deal with every personal scenario. When you're feeling confused and troubled, you can talk to the old guy and find out that he's just as confused and troubled as you are, but it obviously won't kill you. And when you're feeling successful and omnipotent, you can go play squash with the young guy.

Quote of the Day

"You can't trust dogs to watch your food."

—Red Green

Attention Shoppers

I heard a warning the other day about those water pick things that you use to blast water between your teeth. The message was warning me not to use the device on my eyes. I had several reactions to that statement. The first one was okay, don't squirt a needle of pressurized water into my eye area. That makes sense. My second reaction was holy cow, they think I'm a moron. They think that if they don't warn me, I'm going to fire this thing up and try to hose down my retinas. That insulted me. My third and final reaction was acceptance. Acceptance that protecting people from themselves is never a bad thing and not usually unnecessary. Seatbelts and air bags and warning buzzers and smoke detectors and railings and padded rooms are all there for a reason. Besides, having someone assume you're a moron is not a new experience for most married men.

Guilty by Association

I saw an article in a movie magazine about an aging actress and it included some pictures of her in her personal life with her husband. He isn't a show biz guy. He made his money in shoe stores or something. And that may be what created the problem. Because he's not an entertainer, he doesn't really care what he looks like. At the very least, it's okay for him to look old. In contrast, she's had more corrective surgery than Joe Namath's knees. So when you see them together, you think, why would a young good-looking woman like her be with an old dog like him? And how can her son possibly be older than she is? I guess for cosmetic surgery to work properly, everybody in your family has to agree to have it done. All it takes is one wrinkled younger sister and your cover is blown.

Quote of the Day

"I'm not getting smarter, but I'm getting much more secretive about my stupidity."

—*Red Green*

Belittle Be Little

I guess the Space Age is to blame for the worldwide desire for miniaturization. They can get the entire encyclopedia on the head of a pin or something. And everything from phones to cameras to cars is getting smaller. Can we just stop and think about this for a minute? I don't want things to get smaller. When things get small, I lose them. Some days I can't even find my car keys; can you imagine me trying to locate that pin that has the encyclopedia on it? I think they're just making things smaller so we can fit more useless technology into our homes. I say we go the other way. Maximization. Give me a wall-sized TV screen, a great big clunky phone, and a two-foot thick phone book with eighteen-point font.

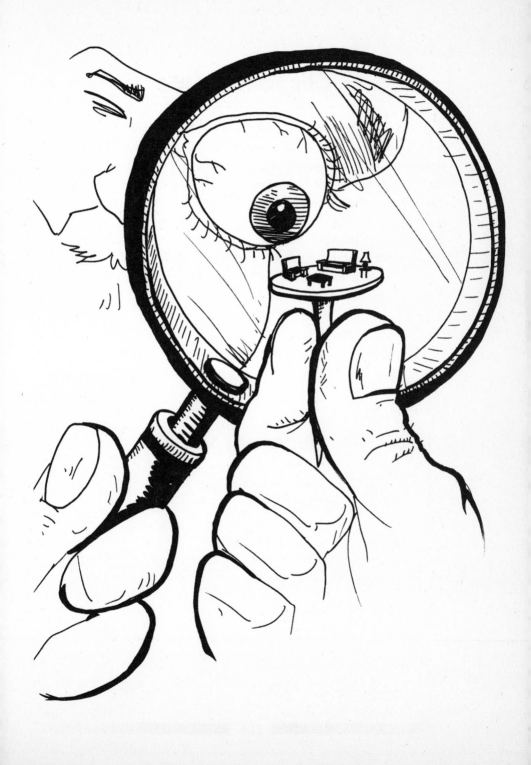

What's Yours Is Yours

After you've been married for a while, your personal belongings tend to get intermingled. Sometimes to save money or because you ran out of something, you end up using toiletries that your wife bought for herself. This can be inappropriate and sometimes harmful. For example, a razor blade that has shaved a pair of human legs is no longer safe to use on a human face. Toothpaste containing baking soda is not for the discerning palate. And you shouldn't be using "Shampoo for Fine Hair" when what you really need is "Shampoo for Scarce Hair."

Quote of the Day

"If you wake up feeling good, cancel your doctor's appointment."

—*Red Green*

Do I Need More Data?

I have a couple of channels on my TV where every inch of the screen is covered with information. One corner has the weather, there's a program in another corner, one section of the screen is devoted to live video of local highways, another to sports, the news is printed in another area, and during all of this, three lines of stock market reports crawl horizontally across the bottom of the screen. Whose idea was this? To bombard me with unconnected random bits of unsolicited information? It's like talking to my brother-in-law. And how did they decide how much info to put up there? Can the average human digest six different sources of data simultaneously? If the answer is yes, then I must have had a sheltered life because I've never met an average human being. Instead of giving me six different things that I don't want, isn't it better to ask me what I want and then just give me that? I feel like I came into the store for an ice cream cone and instead they're offering me thirty-five flavors of yogurt. I sure hope this multi-data barrage doesn't catch on. I already have enough of that kind of chaos going on right inside my own head.

Step Away from the Leaf Blower

Attention Ladies: Men are drawn to machines like moths to a flame. Especially if the machines are broken. However, when you have a broken machine, the last thing you need is a guy interfering who has no idea what he's doing. It's fine if he's your husband or your neighbor because you know they're idiots and you can keep them away. But with strangers, you just don't know. So here are signs to watch for that indicate that this guy has no idea what he's doing:

- He stares at the machine for more than ten minutes without moving or speaking.

- He tells you to shut the machine off.

- He finds a control and turns it a little and waits. Then turns it a lot and waits. Then turns it back to its original position.

- He burns himself on something and pretends it never happened.

- He sprays the entire machine and surrounding area with oil.

- He hides his toolbox.

- As soon as another man arrives on the scene, he backs away just far enough that he evolves from a participant to an observer.

Regrets, I've Had a Few

I know that people tend to have regrets in their lives, and as they get older, these regrets can be very debilitating. You can't go back and change any of them and they can actually stop you from doing things now, out of fear that you'll regret them later. Now, they tell me you must have regrets to be normal, so to keep the real bad ones out of my mind, I've made a list of reasonable regrets that are bad enough to make me feel a slight twinge of guilt, but not so terrible that I end up hating myself. Here are my regrets:

- Buying a car made in a Baltic country.

- Eating that second pizza.

- Not going to the bathroom before riding The Scrambler.

- Not kissing my second girlfriend.

- Kissing my first girlfriend.

- Pulling Grandpa's finger.

The Fix Is Out

I remember when I was a kid we had an old pull-start lawn-mower. You'd tie a knot in one end of a rope, hook that into the hub on top, and then give it a good yank. Sometimes, if your brother was standing too close, the knotted end of the rope would whip out and nail him in the groinal area. That was always good for a laugh. Eventually the knot would break off and you'd have to tie another and then another and, in time, the rope got too short to use. So you'd go to the hardware store, buy a new piece, and start the process all over again. It was inconvenient and sometimes irritating but, on the other hand, it was simple and you always knew how to fix the problem and that made you feel strong and in control. Now, of course, we all have electric-start riding mowers. That's progress. They're way easier to start and do a better, faster cutting job—but on the downside, when something goes wrong, you have no idea how to fix it and that makes you feel weak and out of control. Plus, when you nail your brother in the groinal area with one of those babies, it can be serious.

Bucking the Trend

I have a friend in the real estate business who was telling me how well condos are selling these days, now that the baby boomers are approaching retirement age. He then proceeded to list all of the things that people no longer want in a home, which ended up being a pretty accurate description of the house I currently own. Now, I know the logical decision would be for me to sell my house immediately at a huge loss and go and live in a condo with other people who have done the same thing and then we could all get together on Saturday nights and reminisce about the good old days when we had backyards and parking spots. But I'm not going to do that. There are two things I don't like about trends. First, trends are like breezes: they have to keep moving to exist. So once you start following trends, you're pretty much committing to a life on the road. Second, trends are for the sole purpose of making money. I've always preferred to eke out a living doing something I enjoy, rather than make a fortune doing something I hate. Maybe one day I'll be able to make a fortune doing something I enjoy. But that won't be a trend, it'll be a miracle.

An Ounce of Preparation

With luck, we all get old. But you need to be doing things now, while you still have your faculties, that will make your old age as enjoyable as possible. I'm sure you'll be able to come up with ideas yourselves but here are a few to get you started:

- Get your praying in now, while your knees are still good.

- Make an appointment to have a vasectomy on your 90th birthday.

- Buy trophies at garage sales and scatter them all over your house.

- Make up incredible stories about your life. Nobody's going to listen to you anyway; you might as well have the fun of lying.

- Find things that interest and excite you and stare at them for hours. That way when you're on your deathbed and your whole life flashes before you, it'll be easier to pay attention.

- When you die, leave everything to your deceased parents—one last shot at screwing up the lawyers.

The Big Chill

I was kind of a rebellious teenager, looking to lash out against authority. And I could always find someone willing to take me on. Nowadays I walk away from confrontational people and spend my time with friends. I recommend that instead of looking for people to hit, we all start looking for people to hug. But not in a subway full of strangers. I'll never make that mistake again.

> ## Quote of the Day
>
> *"The best way to guarantee exciting dreams at night is to let your brain rest all day."*
>
> —*Red Green*